101 Knitting-To-Go Projects™

Edited by Jeanne Stauffer

HOUSE of
WHITE
BIRCHES
PUBLISHERS
SINCE 1947

101 Knitting-To-Go Projects

Editor: Jeanne Stauffer
Design Manager: Vicki Blizzard
Technical Editor: Joy Slayton
Associate Editor: Barb Sprunger
Copy Editors: Mary Nowak, Nicki Lehman, Alice Rice
Publications Coordinator: Tanya Turner

Photography: Tammy Christian, Jeff Chilcote, Justin Wiard
Photography Stylist: Arlou Wittwer
Photography Assistant: Linda Quinlan
Production Coordinator: Brenda Gallmeyer
Book and Cover Design: Jessi Butler
Production Artist: Brenda Gallmeyer
Production Assistants: Janet Bowers, Marj Morgan
Traffic Coordinator: Sandra Beres
Technical Artists: Leslie Brandt, Julie Catey, Chad Summers

Publishers: Carl H. Muselman, Arthur K. Muselman
Chief Executive Officer: John Robinson
Marketing Director: Scott Moss
Product Development Director: Vivian Rothe
Publishing Services Manager: Brenda R. Wendling

Printed in the United States of America
First Printing: 2001
Library of Congress Number: 00-109009
ISBN: 1-882138-70-8

Every effort has been made to ensure the accuracy and completeness of the instructions in this book. However, we cannot be responsible for human error or for the results when using materials other than those specified in the instructions, or for variations in individual work.

We had a great time planning this book for you. We know you will enjoy stitching these designs to give as gifts or to use yourself.

First we selected a general focus for the book. We remembered the one underlying theme that many knitters mention to us in their letters. We hear about how much they love to knit and what their favorite projects are. Then they tell us about their biggest problem: finding time to knit.

Bingo! We had the focus of our first knitting book! We asked designers for projects that could be made by busy knitters on the go. Instead of reading out-of-date magazines while you wait to see the doctor, you can knit. Whether you are taking a break at a ski resort, sitting at the airport, waiting for your child to finish practice, stalled in traffic or taking a

short break at the office, you can have more time to knit if you have the right projects.

Many of the projects in this book are knit in strips or blocks so they are easily transportable, even the afghans and sweaters. The texture patterns are easy to remember, so you can start or stop without spending much time figuring out what comes next.

We included smaller projects that can be made quickly. Not all the projects are easy because we know some of you want a challenge, but they are all projects you can knit on the go. So what are you waiting for? There are over 101 designs from which to choose. Gather your needles and yarn and begin!

Happy knitting,

Jeanne Stauffer

Contents

Chapter 1

Home and Holiday Accents

Chapter 2

Finishing Touches

Chapter 3

Kidstuff To Go

Gate 5

Chapter 4

Afghans On The Go

Chapter 5

Spotlight on Sweaters

Home and Holiday Accents

*A*dd a touch of knitting to your home and *your holidays with this collection of projects lovingly stitched in those moments when you are in the car and on the go. These projects may be small in size, but they make great gifts to share with family and friends.*

Chapter 1

Bouquet in a Basket

Design by Sue Childress

Worked in all your favorite colors, this basket of pretty flowers will grace any home.

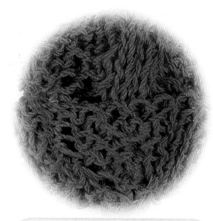

Experience Level
Advanced Beginner**

Materials
- Sport weight cotton yarn (160 yds/50g per ball): 1 ball each yellow, red and green
- Size 4 (3.5mm) needles or size needed to obtain gauge
- 18-gauge floral wire
- Floral tape
- Basket
- Glue
- Foam disk to fit basket
- Stamens for each flower and accent
- 3mm string pearls
- Artificial baby's breath for filler
- 5 yds 2½-inch wire-edge ribbon

Gauge
Approximately 5 sts = 1 inch/2.5cm in St st

Gauge isn't critical in this project.

Pattern Note
Each flower or leaf requires approximately 16 yds of yarn.

Bell Flower
(10 yellow and 10 red used in sample)

Beg at outer edge, CO 59 sts.

Rows 1 and 2: Knit.

Row 3: P3, *k11, p3, rep from * across.

Row 4: K3, *p11, k3, rep from * across.

Row 5: P3, *ssk, k2, yo, sl 1, k2tog, psso, yo, k2, k2tog, p3, rep from * across. (51 sts)

Row 6: K3, *p9, k3, rep from * across.

Row 7: P3, *ssk, k1, yo, sl 1, k2tog, psso, yo, k1, k2tog, p3, rep from * across. (43 sts)

Row 8: K3, *p7, k3, rep from * across.

Row 9: P3, *ssk, yo, sl 1, k2tog, psso, yo, k2tog, p3, rep from * across. (35 sts)

Row 10: K3, *p5, k3, rep from * across.

Row 11: P3, *ssk, k1, k2tog, p3, rep from * across. (27 sts)

Row 12: K3, *p3, k3, rep from * across.

Row 13: *K1, k2tog, rep from * across. (18 sts)

Rows 14–16: Knit.

Row 17: [K2tog] across. (9 sts) BO rem sts.

Leaf
(9 green used in sample)

Note: *Inc by working [p1, k1] in next st.*

Beg at base, CO 8 sts.

Row 1 (RS): K5, yo, k1, yo, k2. (10 sts)

Row 2: P6, inc in next st, k3. (11 sts)

Row 3: K4, p1, k2, yo, k1, yo, k3. (13 sts)

Row 4: P8, inc in next st, k4. (14 sts)

Row 5: K4, p2, k3, yo, k1, yo, k4. (16 sts)

Row 6: P10, inc in next st, k5. (17 sts)

Row 7: K4, p3, k4, yo, k1, yo, k5. (19 sts)

Row 8: P12, inc in next st, k6. (20 sts)

Row 9: K4, p4, ssk, k7, k2tog, k1. (18 sts)

Row 10: P10, inc in next st, k7. (19 sts)

Row 11: K1, ssk, k1, p5, ssk, k5, k2tog, k1. (16 sts)

Row 12: P8, k3, p1, k4. (16 sts)

Row 13: K1, ssk, k2, p2tog, p1, ssk, k3, k2tog, k1. (12 sts)

Row 14: P6, k2, p1, k3. (12 sts)

Row 15: K1, ssk, k1, p2tog, ssk, k1, k2tog, k1. (8 sts)

Row 16: P4, k1, p1, k2.

Row 17: K1, [sl 1, k2tog, psso] twice, k1. (4 sts)

Row 18: [P2tog] twice, pass first st over 2nd st. Fasten off, leaving a tail for sewing.

Sew edges of front and back tog.

Finishing

Cut 1 (8-inch) piece of wire for each flower, leaf and accent. Make a small hook in 1 end of each wire, attach to flower or leaf with hook. Close hook on knitted piece and wrap with floral tape.

Flowers

Roll each flower around stamens and wire before wrapping with tape.

Accents

Make accents with loops of 3mm pearls and with stamens; attach to wires and wrap with tape.

Wrap handle of basket with ribbon and trim with a bow. Cut foam to fit basket and glue in bottom, then arrange flowers, leaves, accents and filler in it. ❖

Thick Oven Mitt & Pot Holder

Design by Edie Eckman

This easy-to-knit project makes a wonderful housewarming gift!

Experience Level
Intermediate***

Pattern Notes
Yarn is used double throughout. Lining is slightly smaller than outside of mitt.

Instructions are given for wool yarn. *Do not use acrylic!* Synthetics will melt against a hot dish and burn the user.

Materials
- Paton's Classic Wool 100 percent wool worsted weight yarn (223 yds/100g per ball): 3 balls blue storm #215 (MC), 1 skein Aran #202 (CC)
- Size 10 (6mm) needles or size needed to obtain gauge
- Tapestry needle
- Size H/8 (5mm) crochet hook

Gauge
14 sts and 21 rows = 4 inches/10cm in St st with yarn used double

To save time, take time to check gauge.

Special Abbreviation
F&B: front and back

Pattern Stitch
(multiple of 2 sts +1)

Row 1 (RS): K into f&b of each st across. (number of sts is doubled)

Row 2: K2tog, *p2tog, k2tog, rep from * across. (original number of sts restored)

Rep Rows 1 and 2 for patt.

Pot Holder

Finished Size
Approximately 7½ inches square

Front
With MC, CO 23 sts.

Beg patt and work even until piece meas 7 inches from beg, ending with Row 2. BO all sts.

Back
With MC, CO 25 sts. Work even in St st until piece meas 7 inches from beg. BO all sts.

Holding WS of pieces tog, beg at one corner with CC, sc around, placing 3 sc in each corner st. Ch 10. Fasten off. Sew end of chain to corner of pot holder, forming a loop for hanging.

Oven Mitt

Finished Size
Approximately 6 x 10½ inches
With MC, CO 17 sts.

Beg patt and work even for 14 rows.

Row 15 and rem RS rows: Rep patt Row 1.

Row 16: *K2tog, p2tog, rep from * to last 2 sts, k1, p1. (18 sts)

Row 18: *K2tog, p2tog, rep from * to last 4 sts, k2tog, p1, k1. (19 sts)

Row 20: Rep Row 16. (20 sts)

Row 22: Rep Row 18. (21 sts)

Rows 24, 26 and 28: Rep patt Row 2.

Divide for thumb
Row 29: K into f&b of next 6 sts, sl these 12 sts on a holder, work even in patt across rem 15 sts.

Row 30: Rep patt Row 2. (15 sts)

Work even in patt until piece meas 9¾ inches from beg, ending with Row 2 of patt.

Shape top
Row 1: BO 2 sts, [k into f&b of next st] 9 times, k3.

Row 2: BO 2 sts, [p2tog, k2tog] 8 times, p2tog, k1.

Row 3: BO 2 sts, [k into f&b of next st] 5 times, k3.

Row 4: BO 2 sts, [p2tog, k2tog] 4 times, p2tog, k1.

BO rem 7 sts.

Rows 3–6: Rep [Rows 1 and 2] twice.

Row 7: BO 1 st, [k in f&b of next st] twice, k2.

Row 8: BO 1 st, p2tog, k2tog, p1.

BO rem 4 sts.

Make a 2nd piece, reversing shaping.

Lining

With MC, CO 19 sts. Work even in St st for 3 inches, ending with a RS row.

CO 2 sts at beg of next 3 RS rows. (25 sts)

Work even until piece meas 5¼ inches from beg, ending with a WS row.

Divide for thumb

K18, place rem 7 sts on holder.

Work even until piece meas 9¾ inches from beg.

BO 2 sts at beg of next 4 rows. Work even for 2 rows. BO rem sts.

Thumb

Sl 7 sts from holder back on ndl.

Work even for 1¼ inches, ending with a WS row. Dec 1 st at each side on next row. Purl 1 row. BO rem 5 sts.

Make a 2nd piece, reversing shaping.

Finishing

With WS tog, whipstitch each lining to its corresponding mitt, just inside edge of mitt. Holding insides tog, with single strand of CC, beg at inside bottom corner, sc through both layers of mitt around hand and thumb. Sc around mitt opening. Ch 10. Fasten off. Sew end of ch to corner of mitt, forming a loop for hanging. ❖

Thumb

Sl 12 sts from holder back on ndl.

Row 1: With WS facing, [p2tog, k2tog] 3 times.

Row 2: K into f&b of each st.

Four Fancy Facecloths

Designs by Edie Eckman

Build your pattern stitch skills with these lovely, portable projects!

Experience Level
Beginner*

Finished Size
Approximately 8 inches square before washing

Materials
- Lily Sugar 'n Cream worsted weight cotton by Spinrite (120 yds/2.5 oz per ball): 1 ball for each cloth: baby pink #47 (Cloth #1), light green #55 (Cloth #2), tea rose #42 (Cloth #3), ivory #07 (Cloth #4)
- Size 8 (5mm) needles or size needed to obtain-gauge
- Tapestry needle

Gauge
16 sts and 32 rows = 4 inches/10cm in garter stitch before washing.

Gauge varies by stitch patt and is not crucial in this project.

Pattern Note
Sl first st of every row purlwise with yarn in front, then take yarn to back bet ndls.

1. Checkerboard Lace Cloth
CO 36 sts.

Border
Rows 1–5: Sl 1, k across.

Beg patt
Row 1 (RS): Sl 1, k8, *[yo, k2tog] 3 times, k6, rep from * once, k3.

Row 2 and all WS rows: Sl 1, k2, p30, k3.

Row 3: Sl 1, k8, *[k2tog, yo] 3 times, k6, rep from * once, k3.

Row 5: Rep Row 1.

Row 7: Rep Row 3.

Row 9: Sl 1, k2, *[yo, k2tog] 3 times, k6, rep from * once, [yo, k2tog] 3 times, k3.

Row 11: Sl 1, k2, *[k2tog, yo] 3 times, k6, rep from * once, [k2tog, yo] 3 times, k3.

Row 13: Rep Row 9.

Row 15: Rep Row 11.

Row 16: Rep Row 2.

Rows 17–40: Rep Rows 1–16, ending with Row 8.

Border
Rows 1–6: Sl 1, knit across. BO all sts.

2. Tile Stitch Cloth
CO 37 sts.

Border
Rows 1–5: Sl 1, k across.

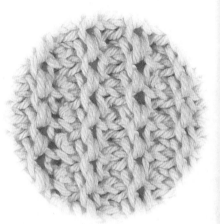

Beg patt
Row 1 (RS): Sl 1, k3, *yo, k2, rep from * to last 3 sts, k3.

Row 2: Sl 1, k2, p1, *p3, pass 3rd st on RH ndl over first 2 sts, rep from * to last 3 sts, k3.

Row 3: Sl 1, k2, *k2, yo, rep from * to last 4 sts, k4.

Row 4: Sl 1, k2, *P3, pass 3rd st on RH ndl over first 2 sts, rep from * to last 4 sts, p1, k3.

Rep Rows 1–4 for patt until cloth meas 7¼ inches from beg.

Border
Rows 1–6: Sl 1, knit across. BO all sts.

3. Mistake Stitch Rib Cloth
CO 33 sts.

Border
Rows 1–5: Sl 1, k across.

Beg patt
Row 1: Sl 1, k2, *k2, p2, rep from * to last 6 sts, k2, p1, k3.

Rep Row 1 for patt until cloth meas 7¼ inches from beg.

Continued on page 40

Heirloom Coat Hangers

Design by Frances Hughes

These delicate accessories will become keepsake treasures for generations to come.

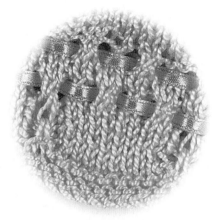

Experience Level
Intermediate***

Finished Size
To fit 19-inch padded hanger

Green Hanger

Materials
- #5 perle cotton: 1 ball (approximately 200 yds) green
- Size 1 (2.25mm) needles or size needed to obtain gauge
- 1½ yds (⅛-inch) ribbon
- Tapestry needle
- Padded coat hanger

Gauge
14 sts = 2 inches/5cm in St st (lightly blocked)

To save time, take time to check gauge.

Special Abbreviation
Knit st 7 rows below (k7b): Drop next st off LH ndl and drop down 7 rows (there will be 7 strands of yarn above st), insert tip of RH ndl into st below loose strands and k1 through st and loose strands.

CO 121 sts. Knit 2 rows.

Rows 1–8: Beg with a knit row, work in St st.

Row 9: K1, *k9, k7b, rep from * to last 10 sts, k10.

Rows 10, 12 and 14: Purl.

Row 11 (eyelet row): K1, *yo, k2tog, rep from * across.

Row 13: Knit.

Rows 15 and 16: Rep Rows 11 and 12.

Row 17: K10, p1, *k9, p1, rep from * to last 10 sts, k10.

Row 18: P9, k3, *p7, k3, rep from * to last 9 sts, p9.

Row 19: K8, p5, *k5, p5, rep from * to last 8 sts, k8.

Row 20: P7, k7, *p3, k7, rep from * to last 7 sts, p7.

Row 21: K6, p9, *k1, p9, rep from * to last 6 sts, k6.

Row 22: Rep Row 20.

Row 23: Rep Row 19.

Row 24: Rep Row 18.

Rows 25–40: Rep [Rows 17–24] twice more.

Row 41: Rep Row 17 across first 60 sts, BO 1 st, complete row in est patt.

Row 42: P60, CO 1 st, p60.

Rows 43–66: Rep [Rows 17–24] 3 times.

Rows 67–72: Rep Rows 11–14, then work Rows 11 and 12 once more.

Rows 73–80: Rep Rows 1–8.

Rows 81 and 82: Knit. BO all sts.

Teardrop I-Cord Tie
Using circular ndl or 2 dpn, CO 3 sts. Do not turn work; at beg of each row, sl sts to other end of ndl and pull yarn across back.

Row 1: K in front and back of each st (6 sts).

Rows 2–7: K6.

Row 8: [K2tog] 3 times. (3 sts rem)

Row 9: K3.

Rep Row 9 for 8 inches then rep Rows 1–8. Cut yarn, thread end through 3 rem sts and fasten off.

Finishing
Press lightly, fold in half lengthwise, sew ends and place over hanger, inserting hook through eyelet.

Referring to photo, weave ribbon through eyelet rows, going through both layers; tie ends in a bow. Tie I-Cord in a bow around hook.

Ivory Hanger

Materials
- Phildar #5 pearl cotton (152 yds/40g per ball): 1 ball ivory
- Size 1 (2.25mm) needles or size needed to obtain gauge
- 1 yd (¼-inch) ribbon
- Small amount of fiberfill (optional)
- Tapestry needle
- Padded coat hanger

Gauge

16 sts and 18 rows = 2 inches/5cm in St st (lightly blocked)

To save time, take time to check gauge.

CO 162 sts.

Rows 1–4: Beg with a knit row, work in St st.

Row 5: K1, *yo, k2tog, rep from * across, end k1.

Row 6: Purl.

Rows 7–14: Work in St st.

Rows 15 and 16: Rep Rows 5 and 6.

Rows 17–34: Work in St st.

Row 35: K80, BO 2 sts, k79.

Row 36: P80, CO 2 sts, p80.

Rows 37–54: Work in St st.

Row 55: Rep Row 5.

Row 56: Rep Row 6.

Rows 57–64: Work in St st.

Row 65: Rep Row 5.

Rows 66–69: Beg with a purl row, work in St st.

BO all sts.

Finishing

Fold piece lengthwise, stitch ends closed. Fold up hem at Rows 5 and 65, whip in place. Place over hanger, inserting hook through eyelet.

Weave ribbon through Rows 15 and 55, going through both layers; tie ends in a bow.

Tassels

CO 14 sts.

Rows 1–25: Work Rows 1–25 of patt as for cover.

Row 26: P2tog across. (7 sts)

Row 27: K2tog, k3tog, k2tog. (3 sts rem)

Work 3 st I-Cord as for green hanger until cord meas 12 inches.

Next row: [K1, p1] in first st, [k1, p1, k1] in next st, [k1, p1] in last st. (7 sts)

Next row: P1 in front and back of each st across. (14 sts)

Beg 2nd tassel

Rows 1–10: Work in St st.

Row 11: K1, *yo, k2tog, rep from * across, end k1.

Rows 12–20: Work in St st.

Row 21: Rep Row 11.

Rows 22–25: Work in St st.

BO all sts. Sew side seams and hem. Thread ribbon through eyelets and tack tog inside tassels. Stuff lightly with fiberfill if desired. Tie cord in a bow around hanger. ❖

Bowknot Table Set

Design by Lois S. Young

Enjoy a new stitch pattern while making this charming table set.

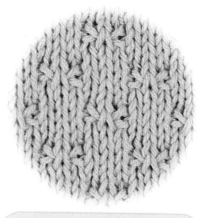

Experience Level
Advanced Beginner**

Finished Size
Place Mat: 20½ x 12½ inches

Coaster: 5 inches square

Napkin Ring: 6½ x 3 inches wide

Materials
- Brown Sheep Cotton Fleece 80 percent pima cotton/20 percent merino wool worsted weight yarn (215 yds/100g per skein): 2 skeins antique lace #CW-047
- Size 6 (4mm) straight needles, 2 double-pointed needles (for edging) or size needed to obtain gauge
- Tapestry needle

Gauge
20 sts and 28 rows = 4 inches/10cm in patt

To save time, take time to check gauge.

Special Abbreviation
Make 1 (M1): Inc by making a backward loop on the RH ndl.

Pattern Stitches
A. Tiny Bowknot Stitch
(place mat and coaster)

Rows 1 and 5 (WS): Sl 1, p to end.

Rows 2 and 6: Sl 1, k to end.

Row 3: Sl 1, p2, *k3, p3, rep from * across.

Row 4: Sl 1, k2, *p1, k1 into st in row below, dropping loop on ndl, p1, k3, rep from * across.

Row 7: Sl 1, p5, *k3, p3, rep from *, end p3.

Row 8: Sl 1, k5, *p1, k1 into st in row below, dropping loop on ndl, p1, k3, rep from *, end k3.

Rep Rows 1–8 for patt.

B. Tiny Bowknot Stitch
(napkin ring)

Rows 1, 2, 5 and 6: Work as above.

Row 3: Sl 1, p1, *k3, p3, rep from *, end p2 instead of p3.

Row 4: Sl 1, k1, *p1, k1 into st in row below, dropping loop on ndl, p1, k3, rep from *, end k2 instead of k3.

Row 7: Sl 1, p4, *k3, p3, rep from *, end p2.

Row 8: Sl 1, k4, *p1, k1 into st in row below, dropping loop on ndl, p1, k3, rep from *, end k2.

C. Edging
Note: When working edging, sl all sts knitwise, and turn work at end of each row.

Use 2 dpn. CO 3 sts.

Row 1 (WS): K2, sl 1, pick up 1 st from edge of article.

Row 2: K2tog, k1, M1, k1. (4 sts)

Row 3: K3, sl 1, pick up 1 st from edge of article.

Row 4: K2tog, k2, M1, k1. (5 sts)

Row 5: K4, sl 1, pick up 1 st from edge of article.

Row 6: K2tog, k4.

Row 7: K4, sl 1, pick up 1 st from edge of article.

Row 8: K2tog, k1, k2tog, k1. (4 sts)

Row 9: K3, sl 1, pick up 1 st from edge of article.

Row 10: K2tog, k2tog, k1. (3 sts)

Row 11: K2, sl 1, pick up 1 st from edge of article.

Row 12: K2tog, k2.

Rep Row 1–12 for edging.

Pattern Note
Sl first st of each row purlwise on RS rows and knitwise on WS rows.

Place Mat
CO 99 sts. Work [Rows 1–8 of patt A] 10 times. Rep Rows 1–6. BO all sts purlwise.

Edging
With WS of mat facing, beg 1 st after corner st on side edge. Work edging along side, picking

up 1 attaching st in each edge st. At corner, attach Rows 1–12 of edging all into same st.

Continue working edging along top or bottom, skipping 1 edge st when attaching edging on Rows 1 and 7. Work corner to match first one. Continue edging in this manner around entire mat. After final corner is turned, BO rem sts. Sew end of edging to beg. Block.

Coaster
CO 21 sts. Work [Rows 1–8 of patt A] 3 times. Rep Rows 1–6. BO all sts purlwise.

Work edging as for place mat, but attach edging to every edge st across top and bottom edges. Block.

Napkin Ring
CO 31 sts. Work Rows 1–8 of patt B, then rep Rows 1–6. BO all sts purlwise.

Work edging along top and bottom edges, attaching it in every edge st. Sew sides tog to form circle. Block. ❖

Experience Level
Intermediate***

Finished Size
Approximately 18 x 12½ inches

Materials
- Brown Sheep Co. Cotton Fleece 80 percent pima cotton/20 percent merino wool worsted weight yarn (215 yds/100g per skein): 1 skein goldenrod #CW340
- Size 6 (4mm) needles or size needed to obtain gauge
- Stitch markers
- Tapestry needle

Braided Ribs Place Mat

Design by Lois S. Young

Enhance your dining experience with the classic elegance of this fine place mat.

Gauge
20 sts and 29 rows = 4 inches/10cm in St st

To save time, take time to check gauge.

Pattern Note
Sl first st of each row purlwise on RS rows and knitwise on WS rows.

Place Mat
CO 95 sts.

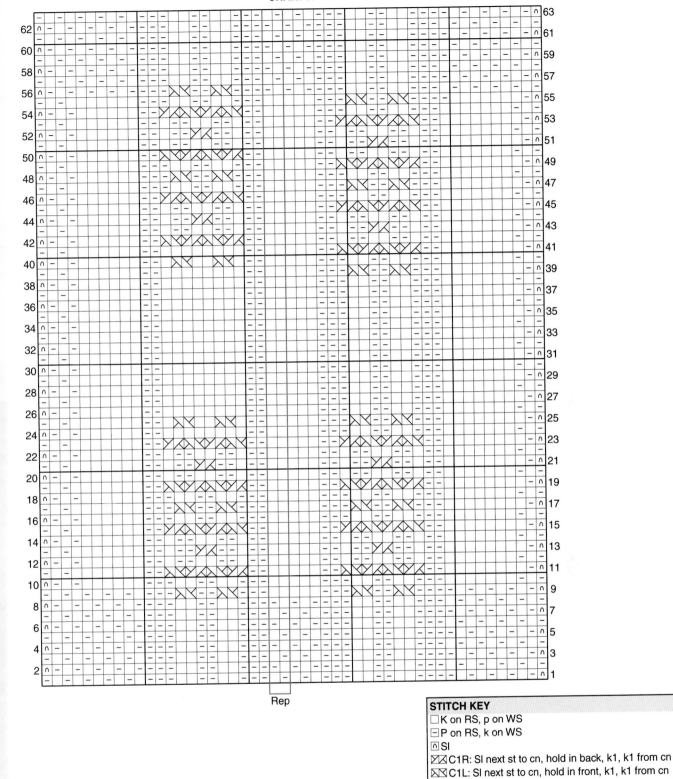

Rep

STITCH KEY
□ K on RS, p on WS
⊟ P on RS, k on WS
∩ Sl
⊠ C1R: Sl next st to cn, hold in back, k1, k1 from cn
⊠ C1L: Sl next st to cn, hold in front, k1, k1 from cn

Row 1: Sl 1, p1, [k1, p1] 4 times, pM, p3, k2, p2, k2, p3, pM, k1, [p1, k1] 25 times, pM, p3, k2, p2, k2, p3, pM, [k1, p1] 5 times.

Continue in est patt from Chart A, working cabled ribs bet markers and keeping center 51 sts in St st bet first and last 8 rows. Work [Rows 1–38] once, [Rows 9–38] once, then work [Rows 39–63] once.

BO knitwise, working last 2 sts as k2tog. Block. ❖

Medallion Table Runner

Design by Diane Zangl

*Medallion Knitting, as named by Mary Thomas,
is the process of knitting separate units to be joined later.*

Experience Level
Intermediate***

Size
Approximately 31 inches
long x 21 inches wide

Materials
• Louet Sales Euroflax 100
percent wetspun 14/4
linen (325 yds/4 oz per
skein): 3 skeins terra
cotta #47
• Size 6 (4mm) 16- and
24-inch circular needles
or size needed to obtain
gauge
• Stitch markers
• Tapestry needle

Gauge
18 sts and 23 rnds = 4 inch-
es/10cm in patt (blocked)

To save time, take time to
check gauge.

Special Abbreviation
Central Double Decrease (cdd):

Sl next 2 sts as if to k2tog, k1,
p2sso.

Pattern Note
Hold 2 strands of yarn tog
throughout project.

Runner
With shorter ndl, CO 74 sts
using your favorite provisional
method. Join without twisting
and knit 1 rnd.

PM bet each section, [work
Rnd 1 of Chart A, Chart B, then
Chart A again] twice. Continue
in est patt through Rnd 64 of
charts, changing to longer ndl
when necessary. Knit 1 rnd.

Continued from page 41

CHART A

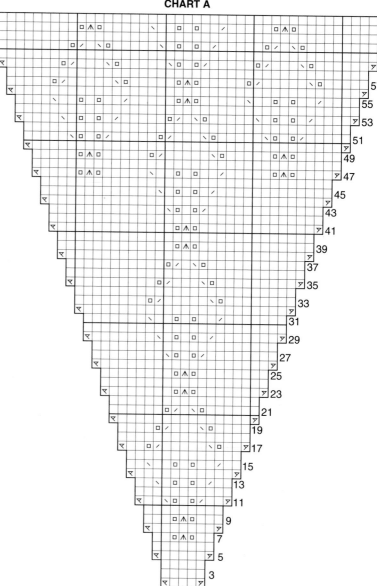

Nautical Place Mat & Napkin Ring

Design by Edie Eckman

*Knit an entire set of these seaworthy accents
for your kitchen or deck table.*

Experience Level

Advanced Beginner**

Gauge

23 sts and 26 rows = 4 inches/10cm in patt

To save time, take time to check gauge.

Pattern Notes

Slip first st of every row purlwise with yarn in front, then take yarn to back bet ndls. First and last 3 sts of each place mat row are worked in garter st with MC.

Sl all patt sts purlwise with yarn on WS of fabric.

Use a separate ball of MC on left side of mat on rows worked with CC, taking care to twist strands at color changes to avoid a hole.

Place mat uses 1 full skein of MC and a partial skein of CC, so napkin ring will require another skein of MC. Designer estimates that a set of 4 place mats would take 5 skeins of MC and 4 skeins of CC.

With MC, CO 85 sts and knit 5 rows. (3 ridges)

Place Mat

Finished Size

Approximately 11 x 15 inches

Materials

- Tahki Yarns Cotton Classic worsted weight mercerized yarn (74 yds/50g per skein): 1 skein navy #3856 (MC), 1 skein off-white #3003 (CC) for each mat
- Size 6 (4mm) needles or size needed to obtain gauge
- Stitch markers
- Tapestry needle

Beg patt

Rows 1 and 2: With MC, sl 1, k2, pM; with CC, k79; pM, with separate strand of MC, k3.

Row 3: With MC, *sl 1, k3, rep from * across, end k1.

Row 4: With MC, sl 1, k2, p1, *sl 1, p3, rep from * to last 5 sts, sl 1, p1, k3.

Rows 5 and 6: Rep Rows 1 and 2.

Row 7: With MC, sl 1, k5, *sl 1, k3, rep from * to last 3 sts, k3.

Row 8: With MC, sl 1, k2, *p3, sl 1, rep from * to last 6 sts, p3, k3.

Rep Rows 1–8 until piece meas 10½ inches, ending with Row 2 or 6. With MC, k 6 rows. BO all sts.

Continued on page 41

Golden Rule Bookmark

Design by Nazanin S. Fard

Try your hand at fine lace knitting with this simple and quick project!

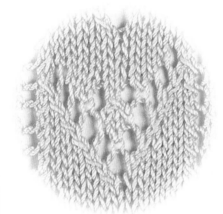

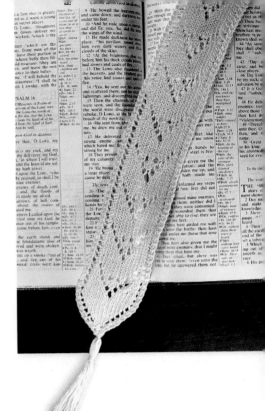

Experience Level
Intermediate***

Finished Size
10¾ x 2 inches (excluding tassel)

Materials
- DMC Traditions 100 percent mercerized crochet cotton, size 10 (350 yd per skein): small amount of yellow #5745
- Size 0 (2mm) needles or size needed to obtain gauge
- 3-inch-wide piece of cardboard
- Aleene's fabric stiffener

Gauge
Approximately 28 sts and 30 rows = 4 inches/10cm in patt

Gauge isn't critical to this project.

Bookmark
Beg at point, CO 3 sts.

Rows 1, 2 and 4: Knit.

Row 3: K1, [k1, yo, k1] in next st, k1. (5 sts)

Row 5: K2, [k1, yo, k1] in next st, k2. (7 sts)

Row 6 and rem WS rows: K2, p to last 2 sts, k2.

Row 7: K2, yo, k3, yo, k2. (9 sts)

Row 9: K2, yo, k5, yo, k2. (11 sts)

Row 11: K2, yo, k7, yo, k2. (13 sts)

Row 13: K2, yo, k9, yo, k2. (15 sts)

Row 15: K2, yo, k11, yo, k2. (17 sts)

Row 17: K2, yo, k13, yo, k2. (19 sts)

Row 19: K2, yo, ssk, k5, yo, ssk, k4, k2tog, yo, k2. (19 sts)

Row 21: K2, yo, ssk, k3, k2tog, yo, k1, yo, ssk, k3, k2tog, yo, k2.

Row 23: K2, yo, ssk, k2, k2tog, yo, k3, yo, ssk, k2, k2tog, yo, k2.

Row 25: K2, yo, ssk, k1, k2tog, yo, k1, yo, k3tog, yo, k1, yo, ssk, k1, k2tog, yo, k2.

Row 27: K2, yo, ssk, k2tog, yo, k7, yo, ssk, k2tog, yo, k2.

Row 29: K2, yo, k3tog, yo, k9, yo, ssk, k3tog, yo, k2.

Row 31: K2, yo, ssk, k11, k2tog, yo, k2.

Row 32: K2, p15, k2.

Rows 33–130: Rep [Rows 19–32] 7 times.

Row 131: K2, *yo, ssk, rep from * across, end k1.

Row 132: Purl.

Rows 133–137: Knit.

BO all sts loosely.

Finishing
Dilute one part fabric stiffener to 10 parts water. Place bookmark in solution for 15 minutes. Blot excess, spread out and let dry.

Tassel
Step 1: Wrap thread around cardboard 20 times.

Step 2: Tie a 6-inch piece of thread through loops on top of cardboard. Leave ends for joining tassel to bookmark.

Step 3: Cut strands at bottom edge and remove cardboard.

Step 4: Wrap another piece of thread around all strands about ¼ inch below top. Tie securely and hide ends inside tassel.

Step 5: Trim ends and fasten to point of bookmark. ❖

Special Day Bookmarks

Designs by Frances Hughes

Knit up a bookmark for that special holiday.

Black Cat Bookmark

Experience Level
Advanced Beginner**

Finished Size
Approximately 2 inches wide x 7 inches long

Materials
- #5 pearl or #10 mercerized cotton: 35 yds orange (MC), small amounts black (CC) and green
- Size 0 (2mm) needles

Gauge
9 sts and 12 rows = 1 inch/2.5cm in St st

Gauge is not critical in this project.

With MC, CO 19 sts.

Work Rows 1–66 of Chart A, working 2 ridges of garter st (4 rows), then work patt in St st, keeping 2 sts in garter st at each edge throughout until chart is completed.

Shape top

Beg on next row, work *k2tog, k to end, rep from * until 2 sts rem. K1, yo, k1, then BO 3 sts.

Finishing

Cut 3 (11-inch) pieces each of orange and black, fold in half, pull loop through yo at end of bookmark, pull snug. Referring to photo, embroider eyes with green. Press lightly. ❖

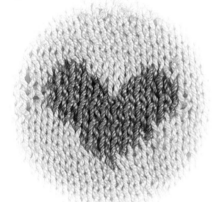

Pink Hearts Bookmark

Experience Level
Advanced Beginner**

Finished Size
Approximately 2 inches wide x 6 inches long

Materials
- #5 pearl or #10 mercerized cotton: 35 yds white (MC), 10 yds pink (CC)

Gauge

9 sts and 12 rows = 1 inch/2.5cm in St st

Gauge is not critical in this project.

With MC, CO 2 sts.

Row 1: K in front and back

of first st, k to end.

Rows 2–19: Rep Row 1 until there are 21 sts on ndl.

Work Rows 1–69 from Chart A, keeping 2 sts at each edge in garter st throughout. On Row 63, change to CC and work rem rows in garter st.

BO all sts.

Finishing

Cut 8 (8-inch) pieces of pink, fold in half, pull loop through bet first 2 sts of bookmark, pull snug. Press lightly. ❖

Bookmark for Dad

Experience Level
Advanced Beginner**

Finished Size
Approximately 2 inches wide x 7 inches long

Materials
- #5 pearl or #10 mercerized cotton: 40 yds white (MC), small amount blue (CC)
- Size 0 (2mm) straight and 2 double-pointed needles
- Boot charm

Gauge

9 sts and 12 rows = 1 inch/2.5cm in St st

Gauge is not critical in this project.

With MC, CO 19 sts.

Rows 1–5: Knit.

Row 6: K2, p to last 2 sts, k2.

Rows 7–12: [Rep Rows 5 and 6] 3 times.

Work Rows 13–72 from Chart A, keeping 2 sts at each edge in garter st throughout.

Shape top

*K2tog, k to end, rep from * until 3 sts rem.

I-Cord

With dpn, on rem 3 sts, *sl sts to end of ndl, pull yarn across back, k3, rep from * until cord meas 4 inches. K3tog, fasten off. Attach charm to end of cord. ❖

Bookmark for Mom

Experience Level
Advanced Beginner**

Finished Size
Approximately 2 inches wide x 7 inches long

Materials
- #5 pearl or #10 mercerized cotton: 40 yds white (MC), small amount violet (CC)
- Size 0 (2mm) straight and 2 double-pointed needles
- Bow charm

Gauge

9 sts and 12 rows = 1 inch/2.5cm in St st

Gauge is not critical in this project.

With MC, CO 19 sts.

Rows 1–5: Knit

Row 6: K2, p to last 2 sts, k2.

Rows 7–12: [Rep Rows 5 and 6] 3 times.

Work Rows 13–72 from Chart A, keeping 2 sts at each edge in garter st throughout.

Shape top

*K2tog, k to end, rep from * until 3 sts rem.

I-Cord

With dpn, on rem 3 sts, *sl sts to end of ndl, pull yarn across back, k3, rep from * until cord meas 4 inches. K3tog, fasten off. Attach charm to end of cord. ❖

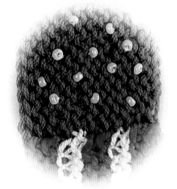

Gauge

9 sts and 12 rows = 1 inch/2.5cm in St st

Gauge is not critical in this project.

Pattern Notes

Flag is worked in garter st throughout.

White stars may be knitted in as you go, or beads may be sewn on when finished.

Beg on long edge, with A, CO 50 sts, drop A, with C, CO 15 sts. (65 sts)

Row 1: K15 C, k50 A.

Continue to work in garter st from Chart A, changing stripe colors as indicated. BO all sts in patt when chart is completed.

Finishing

Cut 3 (14-inch) pieces of gold thread, fold in half, thread loop through 1 corner of flag, pull ends through and pull snug. Sew on beads as indicated on chart if stars were not knitted in. ❖

Gauge

9 sts and 12 rows = 1 inch/2.5cm in St st

Gauge is not critical in this project.

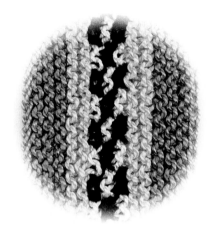

Pattern Note

Bookmark is worked in garter st throughout.

Beg on long edge, with A, CO 64 sts.

Work in garter st from Chart A, changing stripe colors as indicated. BO all sts when chart is completed, do not cut yarn.

Finishing

Insert crochet hook in last loop, ch 24, sl st in 2nd ch from hook, and in each rem ch. Fasten off.

Attach charm to end of cord. Press lightly. ❖

Stars & Stripes Bookmark

Experience Level
Advanced Beginner**

Finished Size
Approximately 1¼ inches wide x 6½ inches long

Materials
- #5 pearl or #10 mercerized cotton: 25 yds each red (A), white (B), blue (C)
- Size 0 (2mm) needles
- 24 white seed beads (optional)
- 2 yds gold thread

Racing Stripes Bookmark

Experience Level
Advanced Beginner**

Finished Size
Approximately 1½ inches wide x 7½ inches long

Materials
- #5 pearl or #10 mercerized cotton: 25 yds green (A), 15 yds yellow (B), small amounts black (C), white (D)
- Size 0 (2mm) needles
- #6 (1.75mm) steel crochet hook
- Key charm

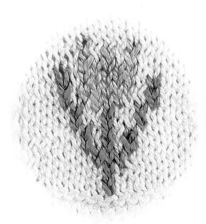

Spring Tulips Bookmark

Experience Level
Advanced Beginner**

Finished Size
Approximately 1½ inches wide x 7½ inches long

Materials
- #5 pearl or #10 mercerized cotton: 35 yds white (A), small amounts mauve (B), green (C)
- Size 0 (2mm) needles

Gauge
9 sts and 12 rows = 1 inch/2.5cm in St st

Gauge is not critical in this project.

With A, CO 2 sts.

Row 1: K in front and back of first st, k to end.

Rows 2–16: Rep Row 1 until there are 17 sts.

Beg with Row 1, work patt from Chart A, keeping first and last st in garter st throughout.

When chart is completed, continue to work in St st as est, dec 1 st at beg of each row until 11 sts rem.

Next row: K2tog, k3, yo, k1, yo, k3, k2tog. BO all sts.

Press lightly. Referring to photo, tie a bow in eyelet hole using 1 strand each of B and C. ❖

CHART A

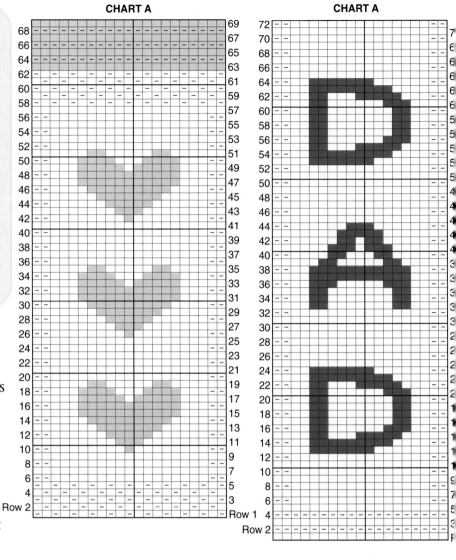

COLOR & STITCH KEY
- ☐ K on RS, p on WS
- ⊟ P on RS, k on WS
- ☐ MC
- ▒ CC

COLOR & STITCH KEY
- ☐ K on RS, p on WS
- ⊟ P on RS, k on WS
- ☐ MC
- ■ CC

COLOR KEY
- ■ Red (A)
- ☐ White (B)
- ■ Blue (C)

CHART A

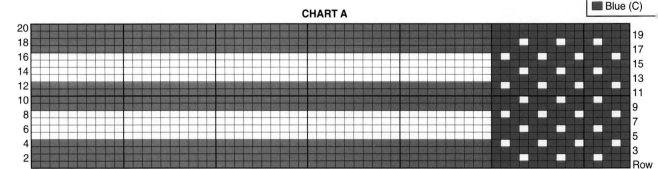

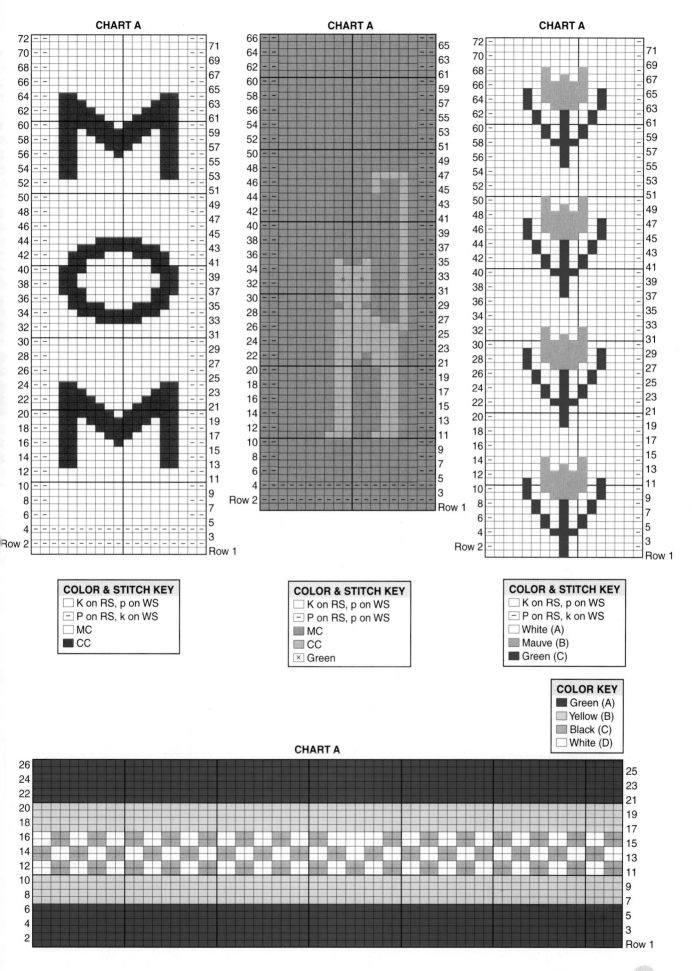

CHART A

COLOR & STITCH KEY
☐ K on RS, p on WS
⊟ P on RS, k on WS
☐ MC
■ CC

CHART A

COLOR & STITCH KEY
☐ K on RS, p on WS
⊟ P on RS, p on WS
▤ MC
▤ CC
☒ Green

CHART A

COLOR & STITCH KEY
☐ K on RS, p on WS
⊟ P on RS, k on WS
☐ White (A)
▤ Mauve (B)
■ Green (C)

COLOR KEY
■ Green (A)
☐ Yellow (B)
▤ Black (C)
☐ White (D)

CHART A

Old-Fashioned Christmas Stockings

Designs by Joyce Englund

Mix and match these designs and borders to knit heirloom stockings for every member of the family!

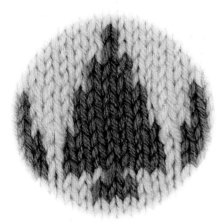

Experience Level
Intermediate***

Finished Size
Approximately 8½ inches wide at top, 19 inches from top to toe

Materials
- Worsted weight yarn: 3 oz MC, 2 oz CC
- Size 5 (3.75mm) 16-inch circular needle
- Size 6 (4mm) double-pointed and 16-inch circular needles
- Stitch markers
- Safety pin
- Size H/8 (5mm) crochet hook
- Tapestry needle
- ¼ yd fabric for lining
- Sewing needle and thread for lining

Gauge
20 sts and 23 rnds = 4 inches/10cm in color patt with larger ndls

To save time, take time to check gauge.

Pattern Notes
On charted section of stocking, mark center back st with safety pin, moving it down as needed so that decs are lined up.

To avoid puckering, carry color not in use loosely across back of work bet motifs.

Borders and design motifs all have same stitch and row count and may be used interchangeably. Letters are 8 rows high; all are 5 sts wide except "I" (1), "Q" (6), and "W" (7).

Special Abbreviation
Central Double Decrease (cdd): Sl next 2 sts as if to k2tog, k1, p2sso.

Stockings
With MC and smaller ndl, beg at top, CO 80 sts. Join without twisting, pM at beg of rnd.

Rnds 1–12: Knit.

Rnd 13: *Yo, k2tog, rep from * around.

Change to larger ndl and knit 11 rnds.

Work lettering
Turn work with CO at top and ndl at bottom. With tapestry ndl and CC yarn, work desired lettering centered in 11 rnds above ndl, leaving 1 st bet letters. Names may be worked on either side or centered on front of stocking.

Note: If preferred, this may be done after completing stocking.

Next rnd: With work in normal position, fold work along Rnd 13, *k1, pick up 2nd st of CO rnd and k it tog with next st, rep from *, being careful to skip only 1 st of CO rnd each time. This covers back of duplicate st letters.

With MC, knit 3 rnds.

Border
Work selected border from Chart A over next 4 rnds. Cut MC, knit 2 rnds with CC.

Beg main patt from Chart A, working patt in MC and centering design on border. (10 patts around)

When first patt is completed, knit 3 rnds.

Beg 2nd chart rep, centering

patts bet first ones. (9 patts around)

At the same time, work cdd at center back at beg of Rnds 4, 8 and 12 of 2nd patt. (74 sts rem after 3rd dec)

When chart is completed, knit 3 rnds.

Beg 3rd chart rep, centering patts bet previous ones, and working cdd at beg of Rnds 1, 5 and 9 of patt. (8 patts around, 68 sts rem after 3rd dec)

When chart is completed, knit 3 rnds.

Place 33 sts on holder for heel. (center back st and 16 sts on each side)

Instep

Working back and forth in St st on rem 35 sts, work patt from chart, centering 3 reps below previous patts. On Rows 3, 7 and 11, dec 1 st at each edge by k1, k2tog, work in patt to 3 sts from end, ssk, k1.

When chart is completed, work 3 rows, then rep chart patt, centering 2 patts bet previous ones, then work 3 rows. Cut CC, leaving a 12-inch end for seam. Place rem 29 sts on holder.

Heel

Place heel sts on ndl, join MC and work in rows.

Note: *Sl all sts purlwise with yarn on WS of work.*

Row 1: K33.

Row 2: Sl 1, p32.

Row 3: Sl 1, k31, turn.

Row 4: Sl 1, p30, turn.

Rows 5–17: Continue to work in this manner, working 1 less st each row.

Row 18: Sl 1, p16, turn.

Row 19: Sl 1, k15, do not turn; without moving yarn, sl next st, bring yarn to front bet

ndls, return sl st to LH ndl, take yarn to back bet ndls, turn.

Row 20: P15, sl next st, take yarn to back bet ndls, return sl st to LH ndl, bring yarn to front bet ndls, turn.

Continue to work in this manner until all 33 heel sts have been worked.

Sole

Work in St st on 33 sts, dec on next row as for instep, and rep dec [every 4th row] twice, then work even on rem 27 sts for 19 more rows. Sole should be same length as instep.

Toe

Join sole and instep on dpn, pM bet sections and dec 1 st at each end of instep on first rnd. (54 sts)

Rnd 1: *K to 3 sts before marker, k2tog, k1, sl M, k1, ssk, rep from *.

Rnd 2: Knit.

Rep Rnds 1 and 2 until 14 sts

CHART A

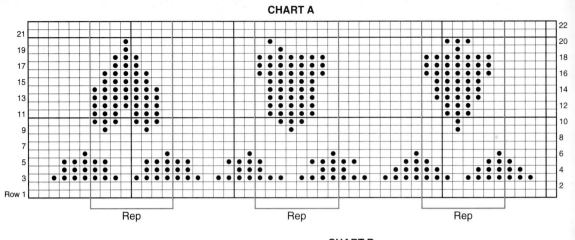

rem and ending at side. Cut yarn, leaving a 12-inch end for weaving toe. Arrange sts so 7 sole sts are on 1 ndl and 7 instep sts are on 2nd ndl.

Weave toe as follows: thread yarn in tapestry ndl, hold ndls holding sts parallel, *insert ndl in first st on front ndl as if to purl, leave st on ndl, go into first st on back ndl as if to knit, sl st off ndl, go into next st on back ndl as if to purl, leave st on ndl, go into first st on front ndl as if to knit, sl st off ndl, rep from * until all sts have been worked.

With CC, seam sole and instep tog.

CHART B

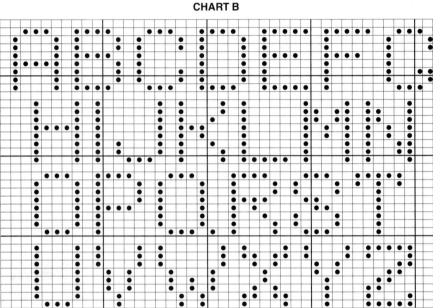

STITCH KEY
☐ MC
▣ CC

Finishing
Hanging Loop

Cut a 3-yd length of MC, fold in half. With crochet hook and doubled yarn, join in yo of border at center back of stocking. Ch 20, fasten off with sl st to beg of ch. Work ends into hem.

Lining

Steam-block stocking before lining. Fold fabric double, mark around stocking. Cut out, leaving ¼-inch seam allowance. Sew seam, then place inside stocking with seam toward stocking. Whip top of lining to hem.

Note: *Fabric lining eliminates need to work in ends and keeps little fingers from snagging strands of yarn.* ❖

Pearls & Lace Pillow

Design by Nazanin S. Fard

Dainty and delicate, this sweet pillow is sure to please!

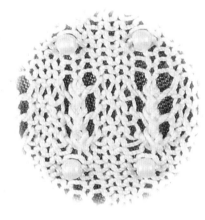

Experience Level
Advanced****

Finished Size
Approximately 6 x 6 inches

Materials
- DMC Cèbèlia 100 percent mercerized cotton crochet thread (50g per skein): 1 skein white
- Size 0 (2mm) needles or size needed to obtain gauge
- 3mm white pearls: 60
- Beading needle or dental floss threader
- Zweigart pink damask fabric, 1 piece 7 x 14 inches
- Fiberfill
- C.M. Offray ribbon flowers, 3 peach
- Gathered (1-inch) lace: approximately 25 inches white
- Sewing needle and white thread
- Aleene's Fabric Stiffener

Gauge
28 sts and 30 rows = 4 inches/10cm in patt

To save time, take time to check gauge.

Pattern Notes
Patt multiple inc from 4 to 6 sts on Row 4; original st count is restored on Row 10.

Using beading needle or floss threader, thread 60 pearls on yarn before beg. On Row 12, sl 1 pearl snugly against st just knitted, continue as instructed. Pearl will be on running thread bet sts.

Pattern Stitch
Multiple of 4 sts + 7

Rows 1 and 3 (WS): Knit.

Row 2: K2, purl to last 2 sts, k2.

Row 4: K2, p3, *yo, k1, yo, p3, rep from *, end k2.

Rows 5, 7 and 9: K5, *p3, k3, rep from *, end last rep k2.

Rows 6 and 8: K2, p3, *yo, k3tog, yo, p3, rep from *, end k2.

Row 10: K2, p3, *k3tog, p3, rep from *, end k2.

Rows 11 and 13: Knit.

Row 12: K2, p3, *sl pearl up to last st, p4, rep from *, end k2.

Row 14: K2, purl to last 2 sts, k2.

Rep Rows 1–14 for patt.

Lace Cover
CO 47 sts.

Knit 2 rows. Work [Rows 1–14 of patt] 6 times. Knit 2 rows. BO all sts loosely.

Finishing
Dilute one part fabric stiffener to 10 parts water, place lace cover in solution. Blot excess and spread out to size and let dry.

Fold fabric in half, WS facing. Sew 2 sides and turn RS out. Fill with fiberfill and sew last side. Sew gathered lace around edge.

Referring to photo, place flowers on lace cover and sew in place. Stitch lace cover to top of pillow. ❖

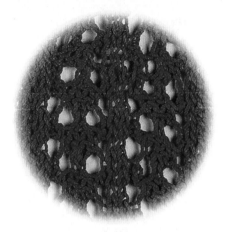

Lacy Christmas Bookmarks

Designs by Sue Childress

Give a good book and a lovely bookmark for Christmas this year.

Red Lace Bookmark

Experience Level
Intermediate***

Finished Size
Approximately 2 inches wide x 14½ inches long

Materials
- #10 mercerized cotton: approximately 100 yds red
- Size 1 (2.25mm) needles
- Ornamental Christmas button

Gauge
8 sts = 1 inch/2.5cm in St st
Gauge is not critical in this project.

Beg at top, CO 20 sts. Knit 1 row.

Border
Rows 1, 3 and 5: *K1, p1, rep from * across.
Rows 2, 4 and 6: *P1, k1, rep from * across.

Beg patt
Row 1: K1, p1, k1, [p1, yo, ssk, k1, k2tog, yo, p1] twice, k1, p1, k1.
Row 2: K1, p1, [k2, p5] twice, k2, p1, k1.
Row 3: K1, p1, k1, [p1, k1, yo, sl 1, k2tog, psso, yo, k1, p1] twice, k1, p1, k1.

Row 4: Rep Row 2.
Rows 5–92: [Rep Rows 1–4] 22 times.

Shape tip
Row 1: [K1, k2tog] twice, k to last 6 sts, [k2tog, k1] twice. (16 sts)
Rows 2–4: Knit.
Rows 5–8: Rep Rows 1–4. (12 sts)
Row 9: [K1, k2tog] twice, [k2tog, k1] twice. (8 sts)
Rows 10–12: Knit.
Row 13: K1, [k2tog] 3 times, k1. (5 sts)
Row 14: Knit.
Row 15: K2tog, k1, k2tog. (3 sts)
BO rem sts.

Finishing
Cut 30 (7½-inch) strands, pull through tip and tie into a tassel with additional piece of thread. Trim with button. Press or wet-block. ❖

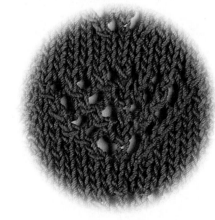

Green Candles Bookmark

Experience Level
Intermediate***

Finished Size
Approximately 2 inches wide x 16 inches long

Materials
- #10 mercerized cotton: approximately 100 yds green
- Size 1 (2.25mm) needles
- Ornamental Christmas button

Gauge
8 sts = 1 inch/2.5cm in St st
Gauge is not critical in this project.

Beg at top, CO 19 sts. Knit 10 rows.

Beg patt
Row 1 (RS): Knit.
Row 2 and rem WS rows: K3, p13, k3.
Rows 3 and 4: Rep Rows 1 and 2.
Row 5: K7, k2tog, yo, k1, yo, ssk, k7.
Row 7: K6, k2tog, yo, k3, yo, ssk, k6.
Row 9: K5, [k2tog, yo] twice, k1, [yo, ssk] twice, k5.
Row 11: K4, [k2tog, yo]

twice, k3, [yo, ssk] twice, k4.

Row 13: K3, [k2tog, yo] 3 times, k1, [yo, ssk] 3 times, k3.

Row 14: Rep Row 2.

Rows 15–112: [Rep Rows 1–14] 7 times.

Shape top

Row 1: Knit.

Row 2: [K3, k2tog] 3 times, k4. (16 sts)

Rows 3–5: Knit.

Row 6: [K2tog] twice, k8, [k2tog] twice. (12 sts)

Rows 7–9: Knit.

Row 10: [K2tog] twice, k4, [k2tog] twice. (8 sts)

Row 11: Knit.

BO rem sts.

Finishing

Fringe bottom edge as desired Trim with button. Press or wet-block. ❖

Angel Bell & Tiny Teddy

Designs by Mary J. Saunders

Worked in the round with I-Cord, these two ornaments will look equally at home on the tree or embellishing a gift.

Experience Level
Intermediate***

Gauge
Approximately 5 sts = 1 inch/2.5cm

Gauge is not critical to this project.

Special Abbreviations
Make 1 (M1): Pick up running thread bet sts, k1 tbl.

Make bobble (MB): In next st, [k1, yo, k1], turn; p3, turn; k3, pass first 2 sts over 3rd st.

Angel Bell

Finished Size
Approximately 4½ inches high

Materials
- Approximately 20 yds sport weight yarn
- Size 5 (3.75mm) double-pointed needles
- Size F/5 (3.75mm) crochet hook
- Tapestry needle
- Cotton balls (for stuffing)
- 1 (20mm) jingle bell

CO 24 sts. Divide sts on 3 ndls and join without twisting.

Rnd 1: Knit.

Rnd 2: *K2tog, yo, k1, yo, k1, k2tog, rep from * around.

Rnds 3–13: Rep Rnds 1 and 2, ending with Rnd 1.

Rnd 14: *K2tog, k1, rep from * around. (16 sts)

Rnds 15, 16, 18 and 21: Knit.

Rnd 17: [K2tog] around. (8 sts)

Rnd 19: [K2tog] around. (4 sts)

Rnd 20: *K1, M1, rep from * around. (8 sts)

Rnd 22: Rep Rnd 20. (16 sts)

Rnds 23–28: Knit.

Rnd 29: [K2tog] around. (8 sts)

Cut yarn, leaving a 15-inch end. Thread yarn in tapestry ndl and run through rem sts. Stuff head with 1 or 2 cotton balls, then pull sts tight and fasten off.

With crochet hook, ch 6, secure to top of head to form hanging loop. Pull end of yarn through head and use to fasten bell inside skirt.

Arms
Working in a ring, pick up and k 4 sts on side of body.

Work 4 st I-Cord as follows: *sl sts to other end of ndl, pull yarn across back, k4, rep from * for 6 rnds. Fasten off and rep for 2nd arm.

Wings
Row 1: Working in a straight line from center back neck, pick up and k 5 sts.

Rows 2, 4, 6 and 8: Knit.

Rows 3, 5 and 7: K2, *yo, k1, rep from * to last st, k1.

BO all sts knitwise.

Rep for other wing.

Tiny Teddy

Finished Size
Approximately 3½ inches high

Materials
- Worsted weight yarn: approximately 15 yds

Body

CO 5 sts. Divide sts on 3 dpn without twisting.

Rnds 1 and 3: Knit.

Rnd 2: [K1, M1] around. (10 sts)

Rnd 4: [K2, M1] around. (15 sts)

Rnd 5: K2, MB (bear's tail), k12.

Rnds 6–10: Knit.

Rnd 11: [K2tog, k1] around. (10 sts)

Rnd 12: Knit.

Stuff body with 4 or 5 cotton balls.

Rnd 13: [K2tog] around. (5 sts)

Rnd 14: [K1, M1] 4 times, k1. (9 sts)

Rnds 15 and 18: Knit.

Rnd 16: [K2, M1] 4 times, k1. (13 sts)

Rnd 17: K7, [k1, yo, k1, yo, k1] in next st, k5. (17 sts)

Rnd 19: K7, k2tog tbl, k1, k2tog, k5. (15 sts)

Rnd 20: K7, sl 1 knitwise, k2tog, psso, k5. (13 sts)

Rnds 21 and 22: Knit.

Rnd 23: K1, [k2tog] around. (7 sts)

Cut yarn, leaving a 15-inch end. Thread yarn in tapestry ndl and run through rem sts. Shape bear's muzzle and embroider mouth and nose with red and black yarn. Stuff head with 1 or 2 cotton balls, then pull sts tight and fasten off.

Legs

Working in a ring with MC, pick up and k 6 sts on side of body.

Work 6 st I-Cord as follows: *sl sts to other end of ndl, pull yarn across back, k6, rep from * for 5 rnds. Fasten off and rep for 2nd leg.

Arms

Working in a ring with MC, pick up and k 4 sts on side of body.

Work 4 st I-Cord as follows: *sl sts to other end of ndl, pull yarn across back, k4, rep from * for 6 rnds. Fasten off and rep for 2nd arm.

Ears

With front of bear facing, pick up and k 5 sts on 1 side of top of head. Work in St st for 3 rows.

Next row: K2tog b, k1, k2tog.

Sl 2 sts, pass first sl st over 2nd sl st, return rem st to LH ndl, and pass rem st over this st. Fasten off. Rep for other ear.

Scarf

With sport weight yarn and smaller ndls, CO 3 sts and work 3 st I-Cord as follows: *sl sts to other end of ndl, pull yarn across back, k3, rep from * for 6 inches. Fasten off.

Finishing

Glue eyes in place on face. Tie scarf around neck. ❖

- MC, 6 inches red and black for face
- Small amount sport weight yarn for scarf
- Size 4 (3.5mm) needles for scarf

- Size 5 (3.75mm) double-pointed needles
- Tapestry needle
- Cotton balls (for stuffing)
- 2 (¼-inch) googly eyes
- Glue for attaching eyes

Pearl Cotton Christmas Ornaments

Designs by Kathleen Power Johnson

Knit a collection of ornaments to decorate your tree.

Experience Level
Beginner*

Materials
- 2 Size 2 (2.75mm) double-pointed needles or size needed to obtain gauge
- Tapestry needle
- Sewing needle and matching sewing thread or embroidery floss
- Small amounts fiberfill
- Size 3 (2.10mm) steel crochet hook

Gauge
28 sts and 52 rows = 1 inch/2.5cm in St st

To save time, take time to check gauge.

Pattern Note
Materials above are used for all ornaments. Other materials are listed separately; finishing instructions are given at end of patt.

Snowman

Finished Size
Approximately 3¾ inches tall

Materials
- DMC Corp. No.3 pearl cotton 100 percent mercerized (16.4 yds/5g per skein): 2 skeins snow white, 1 skein red #349
- Beads: 2 black, 1 red

Following Chart A, with white, CO 7 sts and make 2 snowmen in garter st (k every row).

Scarf
CO 4 sts, work in garter st for 9 inches. BO all sts.

Tie scarf around snowman's neck.

Drum

Finished Size
Approximately 2¼ inches tall

Materials
- DMC Corp. No.3 pearl cotton 100 percent mercerized (16.4 yds/5g per skein): 1 skein blue #797
- DMC Corp. metallic floss 34 percent polyester/66 percent viscose (8.7 yds per skein): 1 skein dark gold #5284
- 20 size 8° gold beads (E beads)
- 2 wooden toothpicks
- White glue

Pattern Stitch
Quilted Lattice
Row 1 and rem WS rows: Purl.

Row 2: K2, *sl 5 wyif, k1, rep from *, end k1.

Row 4: K4, *insert ndl under loose strand and k next st, bringing st out under strand, k5, rep from *, end last rep k4.

Row 6: K1, sl 3 wyif, *k1, sl 5 wyif, rep from *, end k1, sl 3 wyif, k1.

Row 8: K1, *k next st under loose strand, k5, rep from *, end last rep k1.

Rep Rows 1–8 for patt.

Drum

Following Chart B, with metallic floss, CO 21 sts and p 2 rows, cut metallic floss. Join blue pearl cotton and work patt st for 24 rows. Join metallic floss and p 2 rows. BO all sts. Make two pieces.

Drumsticks

Glue a bead on each toothpick.

Round Ornament

Finished Size

Approximately 3 inches tall

Materials

- DMC Corp. No.3 pearl cotton 100 percent mercerized (16.4 yds/5g per skein): 2 skeins green #909
- DMC Corp. metallic floss 34 percent polyester/66 percent viscose (8.7 yds per skein): 1 skein red #5270
- 12 size 8° beads in mixed colors (E beads)

Following Chart C, with green, CO 10 sts and make 2 pieces. Main body is worked in green pearl cotton and St st, horizontal stripes are worked in red metallic floss and garter st.

Diamond Ornament

Finished Size

Approximately 3 inches tall

Materials

- DMC Corp. No.3 pearl cotton 100 percent mercerized (16.4 yds/5g per skein): 2 skeins red #666
- DMC Corp. metallic floss 34 percent polyester/66 percent viscose (8.7 yds per skein): 1 skein dark gold #5284
- 51 size 8° beads in mixed colors (E beads)

Following Chart D, with red, CO 4 sts and make 2 pieces. Main body is worked in red pearl cotton and garter st, horizontal stripes are worked in metallic floss and St st.

Gift Package

Finished Size

Approximately 3 inches square

Materials

- DMC Corp. No.3 pearl cotton 100 percent mercerized (16.4 yds/5g per skein): 1 skeins ecru
- DMC Corp. metallic floss 34 percent polyester/66 percent viscose (8.7 yds per skein): 1 skein dark gold #5282
- 24 inches (¼-inch wide) double-faced red satin ribbon

Pattern Stitch
Seed Stitch

Row 1: K1, *p1, k1, rep

from * across.

Rep Row 1 for patt.

With ecru pearl cotton, CO 21 sts. Work 2 rows seed st in ecru, 2 rows in gold metallic floss.

Continue alternating 2 rows in each thread until piece meas 3 inches. K1 row (turning row).

Continue to work in seed st until 2nd half meas 3 inches. BO all sts.

Finishing
For Snowman, Drum, Round and Diamond

With sewing thread, sew beads in place referring to appropriate chart.

For Diamond

With sewing thread, take a st in bottom of ornament, thread 5 beads, insert ndl into 2nd and rem beads, bringing it out at starting point. Fasten off.

For Gift Package

Tie ribbon around ornament as shown.

For All Ornaments

With pearl cotton, sew 2 pieces tog,

CHART A

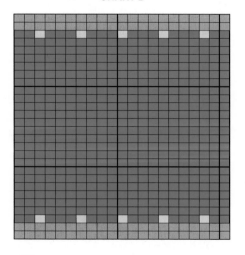

CHART B

stuffing with fiberfill before completing. With crochet hook and pearl cotton, referring to photo, insert hook through top of ornament, pull a loop through and work a 3-inch chain. Break thread, leaving a long tail, and pull

CHART C

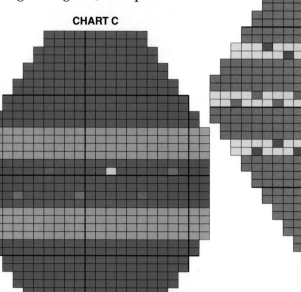

through last loop. Thread tail in tapestry ndl and secure to ornament. ❖

CHART D

Four Fancy Facecloths

Continued from page 12

Border
   Rows 1–6: Sl 1, knit across.
BO all sts.

   4. Granite Stitch Cloth
   CO 38 sts.

Border
   Rows 1–5: Sl 1, k across.

Beg patts
   Row 1 (RS): Sl 1, k across.

   Row 2: Sl 1, k2, *k2tog, rep from * to last 3 sts, k3.

   Row 3: Sl 1, k2, [k1, p1] into each st across to last 3 sts, k3.

   Row 4: Sl 1, k2, p to last 3 sts, k3.

Rep Rows 1–4 for patt until cloth meas 7¼ inches from beg, ending with Row 3.

Border
   Rows 1–5: Sl 1, knit across.
BO all sts. ❖

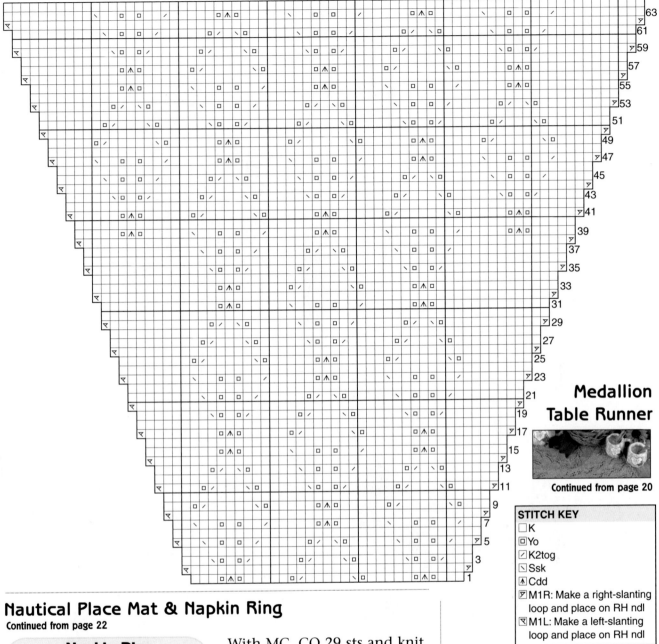

Medallion Table Runner

Continued from page 20

STITCH KEY

☐ K
☐ Yo
☑ K2tog
☐ Ssk
☐ Cdd
☑ M1R: Make a right-slanting loop and place on RH ndl
☑ M1L: Make a left-slanting loop and place on RH ndl

Nautical Place Mat & Napkin Ring
Continued from page 22

Napkin Ring

Finished Size

1¼ inches wide

Materials

• Tahki Yarns Cotton Classic worsted weight mercerized yarn (74 yds/50g per skein): Small amounts navy #3856 (MC), off-white #3003 (CC)

• Size 6 (4mm) needles or size needed to obtain gauge

With MC, CO 29 sts and knit 5 rows (3 ridges).

Row 1: With CC, k1, *sl 1, k1, rep from * across.

Row 2: With CC, k1, *sl 1, k1, rep from * across.

Row 3: With MC, k2, *sl 1, k1, rep from *, end k1.

Row 4: With MC, k2, *sl 1, k1, rep from *, end k1.

Rows 5 and 6: Rep Rows 1 and 2.

With MC, k 4 rows. BO loosely.

Sew ends of napkin ring tog. ❖

Picot Edging

*BO 3 sts, [yo, lift first st on RH ndl over yo] 3 times, insert tip of RH ndl into first st of BO chain and k1, lift first st over st just made. Rep from * around runner.

Finishing

Remove provisional CO, divide sts evenly on 2 ndls. (37 sts on each ndl)

Holding ndls parallel, weave center seam, matching patts. Block. ❖

Finishing Touches

*A*dd a touch of knitting to your
wardrobe with a lovely lace collar,
a perfect-for-the-occasion bag, comfortable
knit socks or an extra-special shawl.
Top it off with a knitted hat or a touch
of lace added to a sweater. You can
knit them on the go and wear
them with pride.

Dr. Jones M.D.

Chapter 2

Slip-Stitch Mittens, Scarf & Ski Band

Design by Yarn by Mills

*This colorful winter set has the look of stained glass.
It'll look great with any coat or jacket!*

Scarf

Experience Level
Intermediate***

Finished Size
Approximately 6 x 60 inches

Materials
- Yarn by Mills washable merino wool worsted weight yarn (130 yds/2 oz per skein): 3 skeins each variegated (A), solid color (B)
- Size 7 (4.5mm) 16-inch circular needle or size needed to obtain gauge
- Tapestry needle

Gauge
20 sts = 4 inches/10cm in St st

To save time, take time to check gauge.

With B, CO 60 sts, pM at beg of rnd and join without twisting. Work in k2, p2 ribbing for 2 inches, then work 1 inch in St st.

Beg patt
Rnds 1 and 2: With B, knit.

Rnds 3 and 4: With A, *k2, sl1, rep from * around.

Rep Rnds 1–4 until piece meas 57 inches. Cut A.

With B, work in St st for 1 inch, then work in k2, p2 ribbing for 2 inches. BO all sts in rib.

Block lightly.

Mittens

Experience Level
Intermediate***

Size
Woman's small(medium) (large) Size is adjusted by changing needle size.

Finished Size
Hand: Approximately 3¼ (3½)(3¾) inches wide

Length: Approximately 13 inches from tip to cuff

Materials
- Yarn by Mills washable merino wool worsted weight yarn (130 yds/2 oz per skein): 1 skein each variegated (A), solid color (B)
- Size 4 (3.5mm)[Size 5 (3.75mm)][Size 6 (4mm)] double-pointed needles or size needed to obtain gauge
- Stitch holder
- Tapestry needle

Gauge
30(28)(26) sts = 4 inches/ 10cm in sl st patt

To save time, take time to check gauge.

With A, CO 48 sts, divide among 3 ndls and join without twisting, pM at beg of rnd.

Rnds 1, 3 and 5: Knit.

Rnds 2, 4 and 6: Purl.

Rnds 7 and 8: With B, rep Rnds 1 and 2.

Rnds 9–13: With A, *k1, p1, rep from * around.

Rnds 14 and 15: With B, *k1, p1, rep from * around.

Rnds 16–22: Rep Rnds 9–15.

Rnds 23 and 24: With A, *k1, p1, rep from * around.

Rnds 25 and 26: With B, *k1, p1, rep from * around.

Rnd 27: With A, *k1, p1, rep from * around.

With B, continue to work in est ribbing until cuff meas 5 inches from beg.

Thumb gusset
At beg of next rnd, inc 2 sts before and after beg of rnd marker, knit around. Rep inc twice more. (12 sts inc, 60 sts on ndls)

Knit 1 rnd.

Beg patt
Rnds 1 and 2: Beg at marker, with A, *k4, sl 1, rep from * around.

Rnds 3 and 4: With B, knit around.

Rnds 5 and 6: With A, *k2, sl 1, rep from * around.

Rep Rnds 3–6 for patt until mitten meas 8 inches from

Continued on page 83

Candles Triangular Scarf

Design by Sue Childress

This versatile scarf can be worn in a variety of ways. Wear it around your neck for a lovely finishing touch to your outfit or use it to adorn your hair.

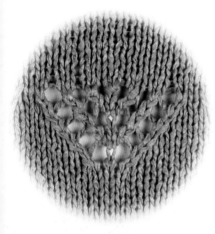

Experience Level
Advanced Beginner**

Finished Size
Approximately 36 x 17 inches (blocked)

Materials
- Katia Idea Mix Knitting Ribbon 45 percent cotton/45 percent rayon/10 percent linen (85 yds/50g per ball): 2 balls light blue
- Size 9 (5.5mm) needles or size needed to obtain gauge
- Tapestry needle

Gauge
16 sts = 4 inches/10cm before blocking

To save time, take time to check gauge.

CO 3 sts.

Row 1 (RS): Knit.

Row 2: Purl.

Row 3: [K1, yo] twice, k1. (5 sts)

Row 4 and rem even rows through 86: Purl.

Row 5: K1, yo, k3, yo, k1. (7 sts)

Row 7: K1, yo, k to last st, yo, k1.

Row 8: Rep Row 4.

Rows 9–14: [Rep Rows 7 and 8] 3 times.

Row 15: K1, yo, k4, k2tog, yo, k1, yo, ssk, k4, yo, k1. (17 sts)

Row 17: K1, yo, k4, k2tog, yo, k3, yo, ssk, k4, yo, k1. (19 sts)

Row 19: K1, yo, k4, [k2tog, yo] twice, k1, [yo, ssk] twice, k4, yo, k1. (21 sts)

Row 21: K1, yo, k4, [k2tog, yo] twice, k3, [yo, ssk] twice, k4, yo, k1. (23 sts)

Row 23: K1, yo, k4, [k2tog, yo] 3 times, k1, [yo, ssk] 3 times, k4, yo, k1. (25 sts)

Rows 25–32: [Rep Rows 7 and 8] 4 times. (33 sts)

Row 33: K1, yo, k6, k2tog, yo, k1, yo, ssk, k9, k2tog, yo, k1, yo, ssk, k6, yo, k1. (35 sts)

Row 35: K1, yo, k6, k2tog, yo, k3, yo, ssk, k7, k2tog, yo, k3, yo, ssk, k6, yo, k1. (37 sts)

Row 37: K1, yo, k6, [k2tog, yo] twice, k1, [yo, ssk] twice, k5, [k2tog, yo] twice, k1, [yo, ssk] twice, k6, yo, k1. (39 sts)

Row 39: K1, yo, k6, [k2tog, yo] twice, k3, [yo, ssk] twice, k3, [k2tog, yo] twice, k3, [yo, ssk] twice, k6, yo, k1. (41 sts)

Row 41: K1, yo, k6, [k2tog, yo] 3 times, k1, [yo, ssk] 3 times, k1, [k2tog, yo] 3 times, k1, [yo, ssk] 3 times, k6, yo, k1. (43 sts)

Rows 43–52: [Rep Rows 7 and 8] 3 times. (53 sts)

Row 53: K1, yo, k9, [k2tog, yo, k1, yo, ssk, k9] 3 times, yo, k1. (55 sts)

Row 55: K1, yo, k9, [k2tog, yo, k3, yo, ssk, k7] 3 times, k2, yo, k1. (57 sts)

Row 57: K1, yo, k9, [{k2tog, yo} twice, k1, {yo, ssk} twice, k5] 3 times, k4, yo, k1. (59 sts)

Row 59: K1, yo, k9, [{k2tog, yo} twice, k3, {yo, ssk} twice, k3] 3 times, k6, yo, k1. (61 sts)

Row 61: K1, yo, k9, [{k2tog, yo} 3 times, k1, {yo, ssk} 3 times, k1] 3 times, k8, yo, k1. (63 sts)

Rows 63–78: [Rep Rows 7 and 8] 3 times. (79 sts)

Row 79: K1, yo, k to last st, yo, k1. (81 sts)

Row 80 (WS): P2, *p2tog, yo, rep from * to last 3 sts, yo, p3.

Rows 81–86: [Rep Rows 7 and 8] 3 times.

Rows 87 and 88: Rep Rows 79 and 80.

Row 89: [K1, yo] twice, k to last 2 sts, [yo, k1] twice.

Row 90: Purl.

Rows 91–100: [Rep Rows 89 and 90] 5 times.

BO all sts in purl.

Wet-block for best results. ❖

Angel Hair Scarf

Design by Frances Hughes

*Add a touch of warmth on a summer evening
with this extra-soft, lightweight scarf.*

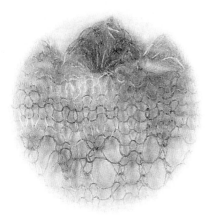

Rows 3 and 4: Rep Rows 1 and 2.

Row 5: K3, *yo, sl 1, k2tog, psso, yo, p2, rep from * to last 3 sts, k3.

Row 6: Knit.

Row 7: K1, *yo, k2tog, rep from * across.

Row 8: Knit.

Rows 9–288: Rep Rows 1–8. (36 reps of patt)

Knit 3 rows. BO all sts loosely.

Finishing

With crochet hook, join with sl st in last BO st, ch 1, [sk 2 BO sts, 7 trc in next st, sk 2 BO sts, sc in next st] 5 times across end of scarf. Fasten off. Rep across other end. ❖

Experience Level
Advanced Beginner**

Finished Size
Approximately 6 x 60 inches

Materials
- Lace weight mohair/silk blend yarn: Approximately 150 yds
- Size 8 (5mm) needles or size needed to obtain gauge
- Size G/6 (4mm) crochet hook

Gauge
14 sts = 4 inches/10cm in patt

Gauge is not critical to this project.

Loosely CO 31 sts. Knit 3 rows.

Beg patt
Row 1: K3, *k3, p2, rep from * to last 3 sts, k3.

Row 2: K3, *k2, p3, rep from * to last 3 sts, k3.

Simply Scrumptious Stole

Design by Frances Hughes

A simple lace pattern with just a 4-row repeat combines with a wide lace edging to produce a beautiful stole.

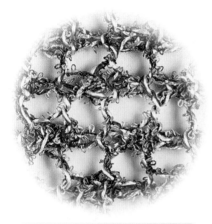

Experience Level
Intermediate***

Finished Size
Approximately 24 x 65 inches

Materials
- Lane Borgosesia Luna sport weight fancy yarn (150 yds/50g per ball): 6 balls #2
- Size 10 (6mm) needles or size needed to obtain gauge
- Tapestry needle

Gauge
4 sts and 5 rows = 1 inch/2.5cm in patt

Gauge is not critical to this project.

Stole
CO 83 sts.

Row 1 (RS): K2, *yo, sl 1, k2tog, psso, yo, k1, rep from * to last st, k1.

Row 2: Purl.

Row 3: K1, k2tog, yo, k1, *yo, sl 1, k2tog, psso, yo, k1, rep from * to last 3 sts, yo, sl 1, k1, psso, k1.

Row 4: Purl.

Rows 5–236: Rep Rows 1–4. (59 reps of patt)

BO all sts.

Edging
Make 2

CO 18 sts.

Row 1: K3. yo, [k2tog] twice, yo, k5, yo, k6. (19 sts)

Row 2: BO 4 sts, k1, yo, k2tog, k3, [k2tog, yo] twice, k1, yo, k2tog, k1. (15 sts)

Row 3: K3, yo, k2tog, k3, yo, k1, yo, k6. (17 sts)

Row 4: K6, yo, [k3, yo, k2tog] twice, k1. (18 sts)

Row 5: K3, yo, [k2tog] twice, yo, k5, yo, k6. (19 sts)

Row 6: BO 4 sts, k1, yo, k2tog, k3, k2tog, [yo, k2tog, k1] twice. (14 sts)

Row 7: K3, yo, k2tog, k1, yo, k2tog, k1, k2tog, yo, k3. (14 sts)

Row 8: K3, yo, k1, yo, sl 1, k2tog, psso, yo, k4, yo, k2tog, k1. (15 sts)

Row 9: Rep Row 3.

Row 10: Rep Row 4.

Rows 11 and 12: Rep Rows 1 and 2.

Rows 13–92: [Rep Rows 3–12] 8 times.

Rows 93 and 94: Rep Rows 1 and 2.

BO all sts. Sew to end of stole. ❖

Evening Waves Shawl

Design by Ann E. Smith

*You'll love knitting and wearing this lovely chenille shawl.
It's so soft you'll want to wear it all the time.*

Experience Level
Beginner*

Finished Size
Approximately 20 x 70 inches

Materials
- Lion Brand Chenille Sensations (87 yds/1.4 oz per skein): 7 skeins denim blue #111 (MC), 6 skeins Venice print #408 (CC)
- Size 7 (4.5mm) needles or size needed to obtain gauge

Gauge
18 sts and 22 rows = 4 inches/10cm in patt

To save time, take time to check gauge.

Pattern Note
To avoid having to weave in multiple loose ends, carry unused strand loosely along side edge and bring strand in use from under unused strand at beg of each RS row.

Beg at lower edge with MC, CO 90 sts. Purl 1 row. Break off MC.

Beg patt
Rows 1–5: With CC, knit.

Row 6: With MC, k1, *k2tog, k2, k into front and back next 2 sts, k3, ssk, rep from * across, end k1.

Row 7: With MC, k1, p across to last st, k1.

Rows 8–11: Rep Rows 6 and 7.

Row 12: With CC, rep Row 6.

Rep Rows 1–12 of patt until shawl meas approximately 70 inches from beg, ending with Row 5.

Change to MC and BO knitwise and loosely. ❖

A Berry Special Scarf

Design by Barbara Venishnick

*A pretty color and a lovely pattern combine
for a truly special scarf.*

Experience Level
Intermediate***

Finished Size
Approximately 8 x 46
inches

Materials
- Cherry Tree Hill Yarns
  Shetland Wool, 100 per-
  cent wool fingering weight
  yarn (600 yds/8 oz per
  ball): 1 ball mulberry
- Size 4 (3.5mm) needles
  or size needed to obtain
  gauge
- Stitch holder or spare
  needle
- Tapestry needle

Gauge
28½ sts and 24 rows = 4 inches/
10cm in berry patt

Pattern Notes
Scarf is knitted in halves and
woven tog at center back.

1 ball will make a scarf up to
approximately 54 inches long.

Special Abbreviations
K5tog: K2tog tbl, k3tog, pass
k2togb st over k3tog st.

Make 1 (M1): Inc by making a backward loop over
right ndl.

Sl2togk: Sl next 2 sts tog
knitwise.

Ruffle
CO 145 sts.

Rows 1 and 3 (WS): K3,
[p11, k5] 8 times, p11, k3.

Row 2: P3, [k11, p5] 8
times, k11, p3.

Row 4: P3, [k4, sl2togk, k1,
p2sso, k4, p5] 8 times, k4, sl2togk,
k1, p2sso, k4, p3. (127 sts)

Rows 5 and 7: K3, [p9, k5]
8 times, p9, k3.

Row 6: P3, [k9, p5] 8 times,

Continued on page 81

Sparkle Scarf

Design by Diane Zangl

A small project with lots of pizzazz, this versatile scarf is a perfect introduction to lace knitting for the beginner.

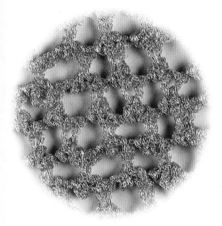

Experience Level
Advanced Beginner**

Finished Size
18 inches long x 40 inches wide at top

Materials
- Berroco Metallica 85 percent rayon/15 percent metallic worsted weight yarn (85 yds/25g per ball): 3 balls silver #1002
- Size 8 (5mm) needles or size needed to obtain gauge
- Tapestry needle

Gauge
8 sts and 12 rows = 4 inches/10cm in patt

To save time, take time to check gauge.

Pattern Notes
Work first 3 and last 3 sts very loose/long to give enough ease to cover vertical spread of lace.

Special Abbreviations
R inc: Knit bar of st below, knit st on LH ndl.

L inc: Knit next st, knit bar of st below.

Pattern Stitch
Knotted Mesh
Row 1 (RS): K1, R inc, *yo twice, k1, rep from * to last 2 sts, L inc, k1.

Row 2: K3, *k1, k first yo loop, p second yo loop, pass 2 knit sts over purl st, rep from * to last 3 sts, k3.

Rep Rows 1 and 2 for patt.

Scarf
CO 4 sts. Knit 2 rows.
Set up patt
Next row: K1, R inc, L inc, k1.

Work in knotted mesh patt until there are 80 sts on ndl, ending with Row 2.

Top Border
Next row (RS): K1, R inc, *yo, k1, rep from * to last 2 sts, L inc, kl. Knit 2 rows. BO loosely. ❖

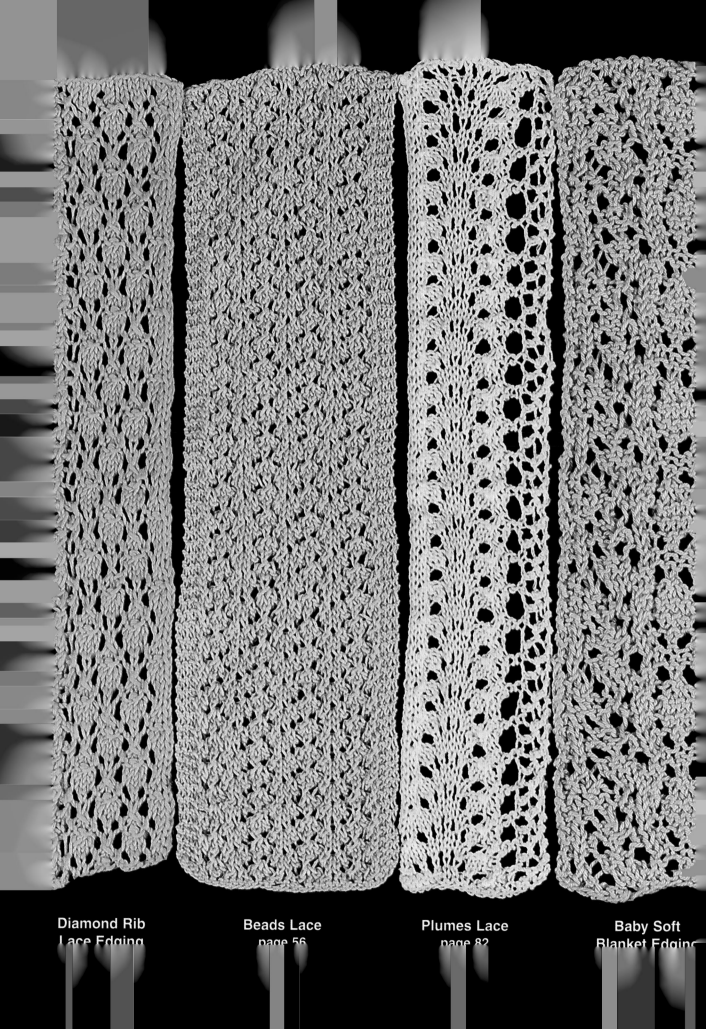

Diamond Rib Lace Edging

Beads Lace page 56

Plumes Lace page 82

Baby Soft Blanket Edging

Designs by Sue Childress

All the edgings have multiple uses from linens to shawls, and each is unique in its own right.

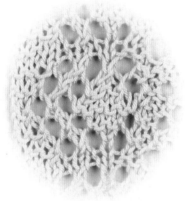

Diamond Rib Lace Edging

Experience Level
Advanced Beginner**

Finished Size
Approximately 4½ inches wide x 2 inches per rep

Materials
• Schachenmayr-Nomotta Catania mercerized cotton sport weight yarn (137 yds/50g per ball): 1 ball blue #0103
• Size 5 (3.75mm) needles or size needed to obtain gauge

Gauge
5 sts = 1 inch/2.5cm in patt

To save time, take time to check gauge.

CO 18 sts.

Row 1: K2, p1, yo, ssk, k1, k2tog, yo, p1, k9. (18 sts)

Flower Lace
page 57

Fan Lace Edging
page 56

Pyramid Lace Edging
page 57

Row 2: K3, k2tog, yo, k2tog, [yo, k1] twice, k1, p5, k3. (19 sts)

Row 3: K2, p1, k1, yo, sl 1, k2tog, psso, yo, k1, p1, k10. (19 sts)

Row 4: K2, [k2tog, yo] twice, k3, yo, k2, p5, k3. (20 sts)

Row 5: K2, p1, yo, ssk, k1, k2tog, yo, p1, k11. (20 sts)

Row 6: K1, [k2tog, yo] twice, k5, yo, k4, p5, k1. (21 sts)

Row 7: K2, p1, k1, yo, sl 1, k2tog, psso, yo, k1, p1, k12. (21 sts)

Row 8: K3, [yo, k2tog] twice, k1, k2tog, yo, k2tog, k3, p5, k1. (20 sts)

Row 9: K2, p1, yo, ssk, k1, k2tog, yo, p1, k11. (20 sts)

Row 10: K4, yo, k2tog, yo, k3tog, yo, k2tog, k3, p5, k1. (19 sts)

Row 11: K2, p1, yo, sl 1, k2tog, psso, yo, k1, p1, k11. (19 sts)

Row 12: K3, p5, k6, yo, k3tog, yo, k2tog. (18 sts)

Rep Rows 1–12 for desired length. BO all sts. ❖

Fan Lace Edging

Experience Level
Advanced Beginner**

Finished Width
Approximately 2 inches wide; each rep is approximately 5 inches long

Materials
- Schachenmayr-Nomotta Catania mercerized cotton sport weight yarn (137 yds/50g per ball): 1 ball yellow #80
- Size 4 (3.5mm) needles or size needed to obtain gauge

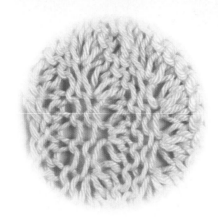

Gauge
5 sts = 1 inch/2.5cm in patt

To save time, take time to check gauge.

Pattern Notes
Patt is a multiple of 25 sts + 2. To figure number of sts to CO, for a piece of lace 14 inches long, at a gauge of 5 sts per inch, 5 x 14 = 70 sts. Nearest multiple of 25 is 75 sts + 2 = 77 sts to CO.

Knitted lace tends to spread when taken off ndls, so wet-block to desired width, easing in as needed when attaching to project.

Pattern Stitch
(Multiple of 25 sts + 2)

Row 1 (RS): Knit.

Row 2: Purl.

Row 3: K1, *[k2tog] 5 times, [{k1, yo, k1} in next st] 5 times, [k2tog] 5 times, rep from * to last st, k1.

Row 4: Knit.

Rep Rows 1–4 until lace is desired width. BO all sts.

For 14-inch wide lace, CO 77 sts. Knit 2 rows, then rep patt Rows 1–4 for desired width. Sample shown is 10 rows wide. ❖

Beads Lace

Experience Level
Intermediate***

Finished Size
Approximately 4 inches wide

Materials
- Grignasco Cotton 5 mercerized cotton (200 yds/50g per ball): 1 ball pink #001
- Size 1 (2.25mm) needles or size needed to obtain gauge

Gauge
17 sts = 2 inches/5cm in patt

To save time, take time to check gauge.

Pattern Note
Patt requires close attention. CO 34 sts and knit 1 row.

Row 1 (RS): K4, k2tog, yo, k1, yo, ssk, [k2, k2tog, yo, k1, yo, ssk] 3 times, k4.

Row 2: K3, [p2tog, yo, p3, yo, k2tog] 4 times, k3.

Row 3: K4, yo, ssk, k1, k2tog, yo, [k2, yo, ssk, k1, k2tog, yo] 3 times, k4.

Row 4: K3, p2, yo, p3tog, yo, [p4, yo, k3tog, yo] 3 times, p2, k3.

Rep Rows 1–4 for desired length. BO all sts. ❖

Flower Lace

Experience Level
Advanced Beginner**

Finished Size
Approximately 2¼ inches wide, 3 inches long per rep

Materials
- Austermann Mirabelle sport weight cotton yarn (155 yds/50g per ball): 1 ball white
- Size 3 (3.25mm) needles or size needed to obtain gauge

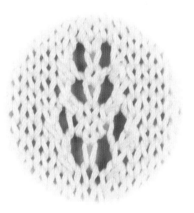

Gauge
13 sts and 14 rows = 2 inches/5cm in St st

To save time, take time to check gauge.

Pattern Note
Lace could be used as an insertion, or add a tiny ribbon to edge eyelets for a special touch.

CO 17 sts. Knit 1 row.

Row 1 (RS): K1, yo, k2tog, k11, k2tog, yo, k1.

Row 2 and rem even rows: Purl.

Row 3: K1, yo, k2tog, k3, k2tog, yo, k1, yo, ssk, k3, k2tog, yo, k1.

Row 5: K1, yo, k2tog, k2, k2tog, yo, k3, yo, ssk, k2, k2tog, yo, k1.

Rows 7 and 9: Rep Row 3.

Row 11: Rep Row 1.

Row 13: K1, yo, k2tog, k1, yo, ssk, k5, k2tog, yo, k1, k2tog, yo, k1.

Row 15: K1, yo, k2tog, k2, yo, ssk, k3, k2tog, yo, k2, k2tog, yo, k1.

Rows 17 and 19: Rep Row 13.

Row 20: Purl.

Rep Rows 1–20 for desired length. BO all sts. ❖

Pyramid Lace Edging

Experience Level
Intermediate***

Finished Size
Approximately 2⅞ inches wide; each rep is approximately 2¼ inches long

Materials
- Manuela #10 crochet cotton (308 yds/50g per ball): 1 ball white
- Size 1 (2.25mm) needles or size needed to obtain gauge

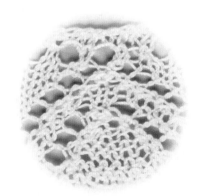

Gauge
9 sts = 1 inch/2.5cm

To save time, take time to check gauge.

Pattern Notes
Patt is a multiple of 17 sts. To figure number of sts to CO for a piece of lace 14 inches long, at a gauge of 9 sts per inch, 9 x 14 inches = 126 sts. Divide 126 by 17 = 7 reps with 5 sts rem. Adjust number of sts to nearest multiple, in this case, 119 sts.

Knitted lace tends to spread when taken off ndls, so wet-block to desired width, easing in as needed when attaching to project.

Pattern Stitch
(Multiple of 17 sts)

Rows 1–5: Knit.

Row 6 (RS): *[K1, yo, ssk] twice, p5, [k2tog, yo, k1] twice, rep from * across.

Row 7: *P6, k5, p6, rep from * across.

Row 8: *K2, yo, ssk, k1, yo, ssk, p3, k2tog, yo, k1, k2tog, yo, k2, rep from * across.

Row 9: *P7, k3, p7, rep from * across.

Row 10: *K3, yo, ssk, k1, yo, ssk, p1, k2tog, yo, k1, k2tog, yo, k3, rep from * across.

Row 11: *P8, k1, p8, rep from * across.

Row 12: *K4, yo, ssk, k1, yo, sl 1, k2tog, psso, yo, k1, k2tog, yo, k4, rep from * across.

Rows 13, 15, 17 and 19: Purl.

Row 14: *K5, yo, ssk, k3, k2tog, yo, k5, rep from * across.

Row 16: *K6, yo, ssk, k1, k2tog, yo, k6, rep from * across.

Continued on page 82

Slanted Edge Lace
page 61

Lil' Bit of Lace
page 60

Scallops Lace
page 61

Sea Shells Lace
page 61

Fern Lace
page 60

The Finishing Touch

Designs by Frances Hughes

Add a touch of romance to your garments and linens with these delicate lace edgings.

Bobble-Edged Lace

Experience Level
Advanced Beginner**

Finished Size
Approximately 2¼ inches wide x ¾ inch per rep

Materials
• Reynolds Saucy mercerized cotton worsted weight yarn (185 yds/100g per skein): 1 skein yellow or desired color
• Size 8 (5mm) needles or size needed to obtain gauge

Gauge
5 sts = 1 inch/2.5cm in patt
   To save time, take time to check gauge.
   CO 10 sts.

Trailing
Vines Lace
page 83

Eyelets &
Shells Lace
page 60

Bobble-Edged
Lace
page 59

Row 1 (RS): K2, p1, yo, ssk, k1, k2tog, yo, p1, [k1, p1] twice in last st, pass 3rd, 2nd and first sts over 4th st to form bobble. (10 sts)

Row 2: K2, p5, k3.

Row 3: K2, p1, k1, yo, sl 1, k2tog, psso, yo, k1, p1, [k1, p1] twice in last st, pass 3rd, 2nd and first sts over 4th st to form bobble. (10 sts)

Row 4: Rep Row 2.

Rep Rows 1–4 for desired length. BO all sts. ❖

Eyelets & Shells Lace

Experience Level
Intermediate***

Finished Size
Approximately 3½ inches wide x 1 inch per rep

Materials
- #10 crochet cotton: 1 ball white
- Size 3 (3.25mm) needles or size needed to obtain gauge

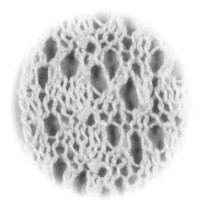

Gauge
15 sts = 2 inches/5cm in patt

To save time, take time to check gauge.

CO 26 sts. Knit 2 rows.

Row 1 (RS): Knit.

Row 2, 4, 6 and 8: K2, p to end.

Row 3: K1, k2tog, yo, *p1, p3tog, p1, [yo, k1] twice, yo, rep from * to last 9 sts, p1, p3tog, p1, yo, k2tog, k2. (26 sts)

Row 5: Knit.

Row 7: Rep Row 3.

Row 9: K2, *yo, k2tog, rep from * across.

Row 10: Rep Row 2.

Rep Rows 1–10 for desired length. K 2 rows and BO all sts. ❖

Fern Lace

Experience Level
Intermediate***

Finished Size
Approximately 2¼ inches wide x 1 inch per rep

Materials
- Steinbach Sissy #10 mercerized crochet cotton (300 yds per ball): 1 ball orchid #308
- Size 2 (2.75mm) needles or size needed to obtain gauge

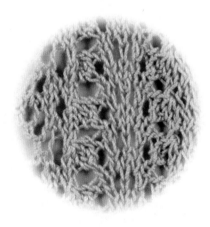

Gauge
10 sts = 1 inch/2.5cm in patt

To save time, take time to check gauge.

CO 18 sts.

Row 1 (RS): Ssk, yo, k15, yo, k1. (19 sts)

Rows 2, 4 and 6: K1, p to end.

Row 3: Ssk, yo, k1, k4tog, [yo, k1] 5 times, yo, k4tog, yo, k2tog, yo, k1. (20 sts)

Row 5: Ssk, yo, k17, yo, k1. (21 sts)

Row 7: Ssk, yo, k1, k4tog, [yo, k1] 5 times, yo, k4tog, [yo, k2tog] twice, yo, k1. (22 sts)

Row 8: BO 4 sts, p to end.

Rep Rows 1–8 for desired length. BO all sts. ❖

Lil' Bit of Lace

Experience Level
Advanced Beginner**

Finished Size
Approximately ⅜ inch wide

Materials
- #20 crochet cotton
- Size 0 (2mm) needles or size needed to obtain gauge

Gauge

Approximately 14 sts and 14 rows = 1 inch/2.5cm (blocked)

Gauge is not critical to this project.

CO 9 sts. Knit 1 row.

Row 1: K2, [yo, k2tog] 3 times, [k1, p1, k1] in last st. (11 sts)

Row 2: K3, pass first and 2nd sts over 3rd st, k8. (9 sts)

Rep Rows 1 and 2 for desired length. BO all sts. ❖

Scallops Lace

Experience Level
Advanced Beginner**

Finished Size
Approximately 1¼ inches wide x 1¼ inch per rep

Materials
- #20 crochet cotton
- Size 0 (2mm) needles or size needed to obtain gauge

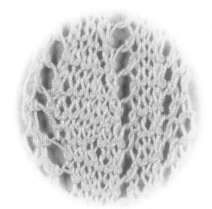

Gauge

14 sts and 14 rows = 1 inch/2.5cm in patt

Gauge is not critical to this project.

CO 13 sts. Knit 1 row.

Row 1 (RS): [K2, yo, k2tog] twice, k3, yo, k2. (14 sts)

Row 2 and rem WS rows: Yo, k2tog, k across.

Row 3: [K2, yo, k2tog] twice, k4, yo, k2. (15 sts)

Row 5: [K2, yo, k2tog] twice, k5, yo, k2. (16 sts)

Row 7: [K2, yo, k2tog] twice, k6, yo, k2. (17 sts)

Row 9: [K2, yo, k2tog] twice, k2tog, k3, k2tog, yo, k2. (16 sts)

Row 11: [K2, yo, k2tog] twice, k2tog, k2, k2tog, yo, k2. (15 sts)

Row 13: [K2, yo, k2tog] twice, k2tog, k1, k2tog, yo, k2. (14 sts)

Row 15: [K2, yo, k2tog] twice, [k2tog] twice, yo, k2. (13 sts)

Row 16: Rep Row 2.

Rep Rows 1–16 for desired length. BO all sts. ❖

Seashells Lace

Experience Level
Advanced Beginner**

Finished Size
Approximately ⅞ inch wide x ⅜ inch per rep

Materials
- Coats Opera #20 crochet cotton (445 yds/50g per ball): 1 ball mint green #523
- Size 0 (2mm) needles or size needed to obtain gauge

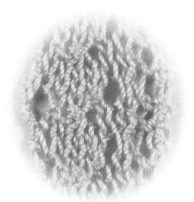

Gauge

12 rows = 1 inch/2.5cm in patt

To save time, take time to check gauge.

CO 10 sts.

Row 1 (RS): K2tog, yo, k8.

Row 2: K1, p6, k3.

Row 3: K2tog, yo, k2, yo, p1, p3tog, p1, yo, k1. (10 sts)

Row 4: K1, p6, k3.

Rep Rows 1–4 for desired length. BO all sts. ❖

Slanted Edge Lace

Experience Level
Intermediate***

Finished Size
Approximately 4 inches wide x 1¼ inches per rep

Materials
- Reynolds Saucy mercerized cotton worsted weight yarn (185 yds/100g per skein): 1 skein light blue
- Size 8 (5mm) needles or size needed to obtain gauge

Continued on page 83

Beaded Barrel Roll Purse

Design by Barbara Venishnick

Knit in mercerized cotton, the added beads add a touch of glamour to your outfit.

Experience Level
Advanced****

Finished Size
Approximately 11 inches wide x 5 inches in diameter

Materials
- Dale of Norway Kolibri 100 percent mercerized cotton (113 yds/50g per ball): 3 balls black #0090 (A), 2 balls red #4246 (B)
- Size 3 (3.25mm) straight and double-pointed needles or size needed to obtain gauge
- 1 Size 1 (2.25mm) or smaller needle
- Bobbins
- Size F/5 (3.75mm) or larger crochet hook
- Westrim Crafts 10/0 Indian seed beads, small package of black, style 145; 10/0 rocaille beads, large package of red, style 140
- 2 yds ³⁄₁₆-inch cord
- Thread for beading, red
- Slim beading needle
- 7-inch black all-purpose zipper

Gauge
25 stitches and 32 rows = 4 inches in patt

To save time, take time to check gauge.

Pattern Note
Body of purse is knitted as a rectangle, then rolled so that selvage edges meet to form top opening of bag. End discs are picked up and worked back and forth.

Provisional CO
With scrap yarn and crochet hook, ch 90 sts plus a couple extra. With A and size 3 needle, pick up and k 90 sts, one in each purl bump on back side of crochet chain.

Make Tuck
With B, WS facing, purl 1 row, turn, knit 1 row. Continue in St st until 10 color B rows are completed. With WS facing, using smaller ndl, slide purl bumps of first B row onto smaller ndl. Hold smaller and larger ndls tog. With A, p2tog, 1 from each ndl. Continue across row, forming a closed tuck.

Beg patt
Row 1 (RS): K1, *k1, p1, rep from * across, end k1.

Row 2: Purl.

Row 3: K1, *p1, k1, rep from * across, end k1.

Row 4: Purl.

Rep Rows 1–4 with A until section meas 2¼ inches, ending with Row 1 or 3.

With B, make a tuck.

Alternate patt sections and tucks until 4 patt sections and 5 tucks are completed.

Circular End Pieces
With A, purl 1 row on RS.

Row 1 (WS): Using bobbins for each section, [p15 A, p15 B] 3 times, turn.

Row 2 (RS): [With B, k1, ssk, k9, k2tog, k1, with A, k1, ssk, k9, k2tog, k1] 3 times. (78 sts rem)

Row 3: [P13 A, p13 B] 3 times.

Row 4: [With B, k1, ssk, k7, k2tog, k1, with A, k1, ssk, k7, k2tog, k1] 3times. (66 sts rem)

Row 5: [P11 A, p11 B] 3 times.

Continue to dec on each RS row in this manner until 18 sts rem.

Last RS row, [with B, sl 2 as if to k2tog, k1, p2sso, with A sl 2, k1, p2sso] 3 times. Cut yarns, leaving 8-inch tails. Pull each tail through last st of each section.

Undo crochet chain on CO edge 1 st at a time, placing each exposed color A st onto larger ndl. With A, p 1 row on

RS and complete as for first circular end piece.

Finishing
Stiffen Tucks

Cut 5 (14-inch) lengths of cord, or length to fit width of tucks exactly. Using a bodkin or large safety pin, run a length of cord through center of each tuck. Anchor in place at each end with sewing thread.

On ends, sew last A section to first B section to close each end. Leave 8-inch tails hanging on outside of bag.

Bead Tucks

Referring to photo, beg at one end of first tuck, attach beading thread to base of tuck on one side. *String approximately 16–18 red beads onto thread, enough to fit snugly over tuck. Wrap beaded thread over tuck and up 3 or 4 sts to form a slanted wrap. Poke thread through tuck at base in new position and pull tight. Secure with a small overcast st. Rep from * until entire tuck has been wrapped. Rep on each tuck.

Note: Designer found it necessary to change to a sewing needle to go through tuck, then back to a beading needle with each wrap.

I-Cord Shoulder Strap

With 2 dpn and A, CO 5 sts.

*K5, do not turn, sl sts to other end of ndl, bring yarn across back and rep from * until cord meas 36 inches or desired length.

Attach I-Cord to center of each end circle, just above 8-inch ends that are left hanging out.

Tassels for Ends

With A and crochet hook, ch 4 and join with sl st to form ring. Fasten off, leaving a 30-inch tail. With beading thread, attach a long strand to edge of crochet ring. *String 22 beads and push them up to ring. String 1 more bead and then insert beading needle back through 22 beads already strung, pull snug. (23rd bead forms end of strand for tassel) Anchor thread in ring. Repeat from *, making a total of 4 red and 4 black strands evenly and alternately spaced around ring.

With yarn ndl, poke 8-inch-long strands left at center of end circle through center of ring of bead tassels. With long tail of ring, anchor it to end of I-Cord, then wrap it around top of tassel to cover joining. Finally, secure end in center of tassel and up through I-Cord. Trim 8-inch strands to finish tassel.

Zipper

With zipper closed, centering it in opening, pin in place along 1 edge. Sew in place with thread using backstitch. With zipper still closed, pin to other side of top bag opening, making sure all tucks match. Open zipper and sew in place. With yarn, sew top seam tog on each side of zipper. ❖

Duffle Bright Carry-All

Design by Diane Zangl

A carry-all for all occasions—use it as a duffle for the gym or a casual bag for that serious shopping trip.

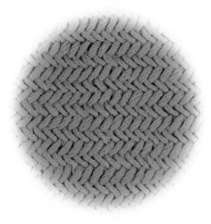

Experience Level
Intermediate***

Finished Measurements
14 inches long x 7 inches wide x 7 inches high

Materials
- Tahki Cotton Classic 100 percent mercerized cotton worsted weight yarn (108 yds/50g per ball): 5 balls persimmon #3411 (MC), 4 balls turquoise #3783 (CC)
- Size 7 (4.5mm) needles or size needed to obtain gauge
- 14-inch sport zipper to match MC
- Matching sewing thread
- 7-inch x 14 inch piece of cardboard (optional)

Gauge
32 sts and 25 rows = 4 inches/10cm in herringbone patt

To save time, take time to check gauge.

Pattern Notes
CO very loosely. Pay careful attention to patt, as it is very easy to lose a st by dropping both off LH ndl instead of only one.

Some sewing experience is needed.

Pattern Stitch
Herringbone Patt
Row 1(RS): Sl 1 knitwise, *k2togb, sl only first st off LH ndl, rep from *, k each second st tog with following st until only one st rem on LH ndl, end k1.

Row 2: Sl 1 purlwise, *p2tog, sl only first st off LH ndl, rep from *, p each second st tog with following st, end p1.

Main Piece
With MC, CO 112 sts. Work even in herringbone patt until piece meas 28 inches.

BO row: Sl 1, *k2togb, pass first st on RH ndl over second st, pick up last st of k2tog and place on LH ndl, rep from * across.

End Pieces
Make 2
With CC, CO 56 sts. Work even in herringbone patt until piece meas 7 inches. BO as above.

Pocket
With CC, CO 56 sts. Work

even in herringbone patt until pocket meas 4½ inches. BO as above.

Strap/Handle
With CC, CO 11 sts. Work even in herringbone patt until strap meas 72 inches. BO as above.

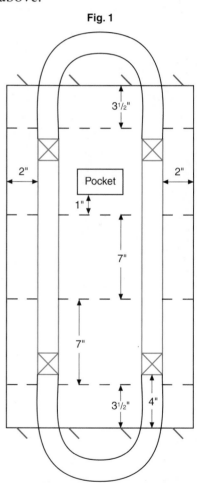

Fig. 1

Sew strap as shown by red lines, placing 4 inches down from top edge and 2 inches in from outer.

KEY	
\ \	Zipper placement
- - -	Fold lines

Finishing

Without twisting strap, sew CO and BO edges tog.

Referring to Fig. 1 for placement, sew strap and pocket to outside of main piece with matching thread. If desired, strap and pocket may be sewn by machine for added stability.

Pin zipper to inside of bag, having one side of zipper on each short end of main piece. Sew in place with matching thread.

With MC yarn, sew one end piece to each end of main piece.

Place cardboard in bottom of bag. ❖

Rainbow Tote

Design by Barbara Venishnick

Carry your latest knitting project in this colorful tote knit in strips.

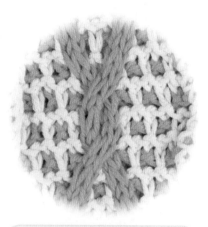

Experience Level
Intermediate***

Finished Size
Approximately 19 inches wide, 11 inches high, 2¾ inches deep

Materials
- Brown Sheep Co. Cotton Fleece 80 percent pima cotton/20 percent merino wool worsted weight yarn (215 yds/100g per skein): 3 skeins putty #CW 105 (MC), 1 skein each goldenrod #CW 340 (A), wild orange #CW 310 (B), barn red #CW 201 (C), new age teal #CW 400 (D)
- Size 6 (4mm) straight and double-pointed needles or size needed to obtain gauge
- Size C/2 (2.75mm) crochet hook
- Cable needle
- 1 (1⅛-inch or larger) button

Gauge
17 st patt strip = 2¾ inches wide
32 row patt rep = 3 inches long
To save time, take time to check gauge.

Pattern Notes
Each 2-color strip is worked separately, then assembled using single crochet to form body of bag, closure and shoulder strap.

Sl all sts as if to purl with yarn in back on RS rows and in front on WS rows.

Special Abbreviations
Cable 3 front (c3f): Sl 2 sts to cn, hold in front, k1, k2 from cn.

Cable 3 back (c3b): Sl 1 st to cn, hold in back, k2, k1 from cn.

Cable 5 back (c5b): Sl 3 sts to cn, hold in back, k2, pass cn bet ndls to front of work, sl 3rd st (MC) on cn back to left ndl, transfer this st, unworked, to RH ndl, k2 from cn. (This keeps central MC st bet 2 crossed arms of cable.)

Pattern Strips
With MC and A, make 2 strips as follows:

With A, CO 17 sts and knit 1 row.

Row 1 (RS): With MC, k4, sl 2, k5, sl2, k4.

Row 2: With MC, k4, sl 2, k5, sl 2, k4.

Row 3: With A, [k1, sl 1] twice, c3f, sl1, k1, sl1, c3b, [sl 1, k1] twice.

Row 4: With A, [k1, sl 1] twice, k1, p2, sl 1, k1, sl 1, p2, [k1, sl 1] twice, k1.

Rows 5 and 6: With MC, k5, sl2, k3, sl2, k5.

Row 7: With A k1, [k1, sl 1] twice, c3f, sl 1, c3b, [sl 1, k1] twice, k1.

Row 8: With A, k2, [sl 1, k1] twice, p2, sl 1, p2, [k1, sl 1] twice, k2.

Rows 9 and 10: With MC k6, sl2, k1, sl2, k6.

Row 11: With A, [k1, sl 1] 3 times, c5b, [sl 1, k1] 3 times.

Row 12: With A, [k1 sl 1] 3 times, p2, sl 1, p2, [sl 1, k1] 3 times.

Rows 13 and 14: Rep Rows 9 and 10.

Row 15: With A, k2, [sl 1, k1] twice, k2, sl 1, k2, [k1, sl 1] twice, k2.

Row 16: With A, k2, [sl 1, k1] twice, p2, sl 1, p2, [k1, sl 1] twice, k2.

Rows 17 and 18: Rep Rows 9 and 10.

Rows 19 and 20: Rep Rows 11 and 12.

Rows 21 and 22: Rep Rows 9 and 10.

Row 23: With A, k1, [k1, sl 1] twice, c3b, sl 1, c3f, [sl 1, k1] twice, k1.

Row 24: With A, k1, [k1, sl 1] twice, p2, k1, sl 1, k1, p2,

[sl 1, k1] twice, k1.

Rows 25 and 26: Rep Rows 5 and 6.

Row 27: With A, [k1, sl 1] twice, c3b, sl 1, k1, sl 1, c3f, [sl 1, k1] twice.

Row 28: With A, [k1, sl 1] twice, p2, [k1, sl 1] twice, k1, p2, [sl 1, k1] twice.

Rows 29 and 30: Rep Rows 1 and 2.

Row 31: With A, k2, sl 1, k3, [sl 1, k1] twice, sl 1, k3, sl 1, k2.

Row 32: With A, k2, sl 1, k1, p2, [sl 1, k1] twice, sl 1, p2, k1, sl 1, k2.

[Rep Rows 1–32] 7 times more. With RS facing and A, BO all sts.

Make 2 strips each in same way, using MC and B and MC and C.

Center strip and flap

With MC and D, work [Rows 1–32] 9 times, then work [Rows 1–8] once more. Leave sts on ndl.

Make Loop

With A and RS facing, BO 6 sts, k1, k2tog, k7. Turn and BO 6 sts. Transfer rem 4 sts to dpn. Work I-Cord as follows: *K4, do not turn, sl sts to other end of ndl, bring yarn across back and rep from * until cord meas 3 inches.

BO 4 sts, fold I-Cord in half to form loop and sew to WS of flap.

Sides and Shoulder Strap

With MC and D, work [Rows 1–32] 16 times. BO all sts.

Finishing

Referring to Fig. 1, hold 1 A strip and 1 B strip with WS tog, using MC and crochet hook, join by working 1 sc bet each garter ridge of patt st. Join 1 C strip to other side of B strip in same way. Join central D strip to C strip, leaving extra 1½ reps free at back edge of bag. Continue in this manner, adding 2nd C, B and A strips

to those already assembled.

Center each end of long D strip at middle of A strip on each side of bag. Fold bag up on each side of this strip, forming front, back and bottom of bag. Crochet along each of these edges as for joining of strips, forming sides of bag.

With RS of front facing, using MC, pick up and k 112 sts [16 sts in each section] along top edge. Turn and knit 2 rows. Work 3 more rows in St st. BO in knit with RS facing. Fold facing to inside of bag and sew in place.

With RS of back edge of bag facing, pick up and k 48 sts along top edges of 3 strips on 1 side of center flap. Work facing as for front. Rep on other side of center flap.

With MC work 1 row of sc along each side edge of shoulder strap, and each side of front flap. Sew on button. ❖

FIG. 1

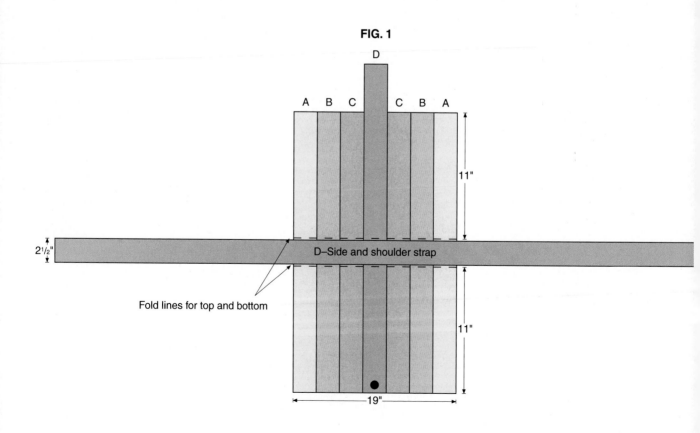

D

A B C   C B A

11"

2½"

D—Side and shoulder strap

Fold lines for top and bottom

11"

19"

Pretty Petals Collar

Design by Barbara Venishnick

Quick-to-knit little petals join to create a cute spring collar.
Overlapping petals make it easy to adjust to fit your neckline.

Petal

Make 9

CO 50 sts and knit 2 rows.

Row 1(RS): K16, k2tog, k5, k2tog, ssk, k5, ssk, k16.

Row 2 and rem WS rows: Purl.

Row 3: K13, k2tog, yo, k2tog, k4, k2tog, ssk, k4, ssk, yo, ssk, k13.

Row 5: K12, k2tog, yo, k2tog, k3, k2tog, ssk, k3, ssk, yo, ssk, k12.

Row 7: K11, k2tog, yo, k2tog, k2, k2tog, ssk, k2, ssk, yo, ssk, k11.

Row 9: K10, k2tog, yo, k2tog, k1, k2tog, ssk, k1, ssk, yo, ssk, k10.

Row 11: K9, k2tog, yo, [k2tog] twice, [ssk] twice, yo, ssk, k9.

Continued on page 81

Experience Level

Intermediate***

Finished Size

20 inches at neckline; each petal meas 4½ inches wide and 4 inches high

Materials

- Berroco Cotton Twist 70 percent mercerized cotton/30 percent rayon DK weight yarn (85 yds/50g per hank): 2 hanks color #8385
- Size 4 (3.5mm) needles or size needed to obtain gauge
- 1 (⅜-inch/10mm) pearl bead
- Size C/2 (2.75mm) crochet hook
- Tapestry needle

Gauge

22 sts and 30 rows = 4 inches/10cm in St st

To save time, take time to check gauge.

Annie Oakley Collar

Design by Barbara Venishnick

Here's the perfect finishing touch for a plain sweater or top. It looks just as lovely with a casual knit dress as with a sporty top.

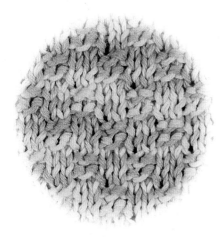

Experience Level
Intermediate***

Finished Size
14 inches wide x 17 inches deep, plus ties

Materials
- Brown Sheep Co. Kaleidoscope 80 percent pima cotton/20 percent merino wool worsted weight yarn (107 yds/50g per skein): 3 skeins Nome #KAL 60 (A)
- Brown Sheep Co. Cotton Fleece 80 percent pima cotton/20 percent merino wool worsted weight yarn (215 yds/100g per skein): 1 skein putty #CW 105 (B)
- Size 5 (3.75mm) needles or size needed to obtain gauge
- Stitch holder
- Tapestry needle

Gauge
20 stitches and 32 rows = 4 inches/10cm in patt

To save time, take time to check gauge.

Special Abbreviation
Make 1 (M1): Inc by making a backward loop over right ndl.

Collar
Beg at lower back, with A, CO 70 sts. Work in patt as follows:

Rows 1 and 3 (RS): *K2, p2, rep from * across, end k2.

Row 2 and all WS rows: Purl.

Rows 5 and 7: *P2, k2, rep from * across, end p2.

Row 8: Purl.

Rep Rows 1–8 until back of collar meas 7 inches from CO edge.

Divide for back neck opening
With RS facing, work in est patt across 20 sts, place 30 sts on holder for back neck, join new ball and work in patt across rem 20 sts.

Beg facings
P20 sts, CO 7 sts [for facing]; on other side of opening, CO 7 sts, purl across.

Next row: Work 20 sts in est patt, sl 1, k6; k6, sl 1, work 20 sts in est patt.

Next row: Purl all sts.

Continue in this manner, sl 1 st at neck edge as above every RS row, working facing in St st and body of collar in patt. After 4 rows, inc as follows: right side, patt 20, M1, sl 1, k6; left side, k6, sl 1, M1, patt 20. On WS, purl across.

Continue to work as est, inc 1 st on each side of neck opening [every 4th row] 12 more times, until there are 40 sts on each half of front. When collar meas 14 inches from CO edge, at beg of next 2 rows, BO 27 sts for bottom front edge of collar; 13 sts rem on each side.

Ties
With RS facing, work in est patt over 6 sts, sl 1, patt over 6 sts from facing; on other side, patt over 6 sts, sl 1, patt over 6 sts. On WS, purl all sts.

Continue working all sts in patt, sl center st every RS row, M1 on each side of sl st [every 8th row] 6 times. Purl 1 row even on all 25 sts of each tie.

BO 2 sts at beg of next 12 rows on each tie. Pull yarn through last center st, cut yarn leaving a long tail.

Fold ties in half along sl st edge. Using long tail, sew along BO edge and up sides of ties to base of collar.

Back neck facing
Return 30 back neck sts to ndls, with WS facing, CO 7 sts, p7, k30 neck sts, CO 7 more sts at end of row. Turn and k44.

Continue in St st until facing is 1 inch deep. BO loosely.

Sew 7 CO sts of side facing to

7 CO sts of back neck facing on each side. Sew facing to inside of collar all around neck opening.

Fringe Trim

With B, CO 7 sts

Row 1 (RS): K3, yo, k2tog, k2.

Row 2: P4, yo, p2tog, p1.

Rep Rows 1 and 2 until strip meas 56 inches, or long enough to fit all around outer edge of collar. With RS facing, BO 4 sts, pull yarn through 5th st, 2 sts rem. Unravel these 2 sts all way down to form a looped fringe.

Finishing

Pin trim evenly to outside edge of collar, making neat folds at each corner. Allow only looped fringe to extend over edge. Sew in place at edge of collar and at top of trim.

Slide

With B, CO 15 sts. Work in St st for ¾ inch, purl 1 row on RS, work in St st for 1½ inches, purl 1 row on RS, St st for another ¾ inch. BO all sts. Sew sides tog to form a tube. Turn tube inside out. Fold top and bottom facings in toward center along purl ridges. Sew CO to BO edge. Turn tube right side out.

Press collar and push slide over both ties. Fringe may be cut or left as loops. ❖

Lace Leaf Socks

Design by E. J. Slayton

Keep your toes warm and comfy in these hand-knit socks.
You'll want to make several pairs in your favorite colors.

Experience Level
Advanced Beginner**

Size
Women's small/medium (large) Instructions are given for smaller size, with larger size in parentheses. When only 1 number is given, it applies to both sizes.

Finished Measurements
Top: 7½(8) inches
Foot length: 9¼(10) inches

Materials
- Froelich Wolle's Sedrun 90 percent wool/10 percent nylon sport weight yarn (131 yds/50g per skein): 2(3) skeins #5547
- Size 3 (3.25mm) double-pointed needles or size needed to obtain gauge
- Heel and toe reinforcement (optional)
- Stitch markers
- Safety pin
- Tapestry needle

Gauge
13 sts and 16 rnds = 2 inches/ 5cm in St st

To save time, take time to check gauge.

Special Abbreviation
Make 1 (M1): Inc by making a backward loop over the right ndl.

Sock
CO 48(52) sts. Join, being careful not to twist and work in k2, p2 ribbing for 2 inches.

Set up patt
M0(1), k0(1), p1(2), [k3, p2] 4 times, pM, k2, M1, k3, pM, [p2, k3] 4 times, p1(2), k0(1). Sl first st to Ndl 3(last st to Ndl 1) so Ndl 1 beg with k3.

Rnd 1: *Pass st 3 over first 2 sts, k1, yo, k1, p2 *, rep from * to marker, k2tog, k1, [yo, k1] twice, ssk, p2, rep bet * * to end of rnd.

Rnds 2, 4, 6 and 8: *K3, p2 *, rep from * to marker, k7, p2, rep bet * * to end of rnd.

Rnd 3: *K3, p2 *, rep from * to marker, k2tog, yo, k3, yo, ssk, p2, rep bet * * to end of rnd.

Rnd 5: *Pass st 3 over first 2 sts, k1, yo, k1, p2 *, rep from * to marker, k1, yo, ssk, k1, k2tog, yo, k1, p2, rep bet * * to end of rnd.

Rnd 7: *K3, p2 *, rep from * to marker, k2, yo, sl 2, k1, p2sso, yo, k2, p2, rep bet * * to end of rnd.

Rep Rnds 1–8 for patt until top meas 7½(8) inches or desired length.

Heel
K across next 11(15) sts; divide next 25(27) sts centered on leaf patt on 2 ndls for instep; sl rem 13(12) sts to beg of first ndl. Turn and p across, inc 1(0) in center. (25, 27 heel sts)

Row 1 (RS): sl 1, *k1, sl 1, rep from * across.

Row 2: Purl.

Rows 3–23(25): Rep Rows 1 and 2, ending with Row 1.

Shape heel
Place safety pin marker in st #13(14). Shaping takes place evenly spaced on each side of this center st.

Row 1 (WS): P15(16), p2tog, p1, turn.

CHART A

			−	−				−	−						o	⅄	o					−	−				−	−				
			−	−	c	ᗤ	ᗤ	−	−							o	╱		╲	o			−	−	c	ᗤ	ᗤ	−	−					7
			−	−				−	−					o	╱				╲	o		−	−				−	−					5
			−	−	c	ᗤ	ᗤ	−	−				╲	o					o	╱		−	−	c	ᗤ	ᗤ	−	−					3
			−	−				−	−			╲		o					o		╱	−	−				−	−					1

STITCH KEY
- ☐ K
- − P
- o Yo
- ╱ K2tog
- ╲ Ssk
- ⅄ Sl2, k1, p2sso
- c ᗤ ᗤ Pass st 3 over first 2 sts, k1, yo, k1

before dec each row until all sts have been worked, ending with a RS row. (15, 17 sts rem)

Instep

Using ndl containing rem heel sts, pick up and k 12(13) sts in loops along edge of heel flap (Ndl 1); with free ndl, k2(3), pM, work in patt across 21 sts, pM, k2(3) (25, 27 instep sts on Ndl 2); pick up and k 12(13) sts in loops along edge of heel flap, with same ndl, k7(8) sts from Ndl 1 (19, 21 sts on Ndl 3). (64, 70 sts)

Rnd 1: K to marker, work 21 sts in est patt, k to end.

Rnd 2: K to last 3 sts on Ndl 1, k2tog, k1; work across Ndl 2 in est patt; at beg of Ndl 3, k1, ssk, k to end.

Rep Rnds 1 and 2 until a total of 25(27) sts rem on Ndls 1 and 3, then work even in est patt until foot meas 7¼(8) inches or approximately 2 inches less than desired length.

Toe

Rnd 1: Knit.

Rnd 2: K to last 3 sts on Ndl 1, k2tog, k1; on Ndl 2, k1, ssk, k to last 3 sts, k2tog, k1; on Ndl 3, k1, ssk, k to end.

Rep Rnds 1 and 2 until 22 sts rem (all sizes). With Ndl 3, k across sts from Ndl 1. (11 sts each on 2 ndls)

Weave toe

Cut yarn, leaving an 18-inch end. Thread yarn in tapestry ndl, hold ndls holding sts parallel, *insert ndl in first st on front ndl as if to purl, leave st on ndl, go into first st on back ndl as if to knit, sl st off ndl, go into next st on back ndl as if to purl, leave st on ndl, go into first st on front ndl as if to knit, sl st off ndl, rep from * until all sts have been worked. ❖

Row 2: sl 1, k6, k2tog, k1, turn.

Row 3: sl 1, p7, p2tog, p1, turn.

Row 4: sl 1, k8, k2tog, k1, turn.

Continue to work in this manner, having 1 more st

Alberta Clipper Boot Socks

Design by E. J. Slayton

Keep those toes toasty when tromping the trails next winter! These socks are easy to make and comfortable to wear!

Experience Level
Advanced Beginner**

Size
Adult small(medium) (large) Instructions are given for smallest size, with larger sizes in parentheses. When only 1 number is given, it applies to all sizes.

Finished Measurements
Cuff: 8½(9)(9½) inches
Foot length: 9(10)(11) inches

Materials
- Brown Sheep Co. Nature Spun worsted weight yarn (245 yds/100g per skein): 1(1)(2) skeins ash #720 (MC), 1 skein Harlan's forest, #19 (CC)
- Size 4 (3.5mm) double-pointed needles
- Heel and toe reinforcement or Wooly Nylon to match CC (optional)
- Stitch markers
- Safety pin
- Tapestry needle

Gauge
11 sts and 16 rnds = 2 inches/5 cm in St st in rnds

To save time, take time to check gauge.

Pattern Stitch
Seed St Rib (multiple of 5 sts)

Rnd 1: *K3, p2, rep from * around.

Rnd 2: *K1, p1, k1, p2, rep from * around.

Rep Rnds 1 and 2 for patt.

Boot Socks
With MC, CO 45(50)(55) sts. Divide sts on 3 ndls and join, being careful not to twist. Work in k3, p2 ribbing for 2(2½)(2½) inches.

Attach CC and knit 1 rnd, then work 4 rnds in seed st rib patt. Cut CC.

With MC, knit 1 rnd. Beg with Rnd 2, work in seed st rib patt until sock top meas 7½(8½)(8½) inches or desired length.

Heel
Knit across next 10(14)(13) sts, break MC, attach CC and turn. P10(14)(13), then with same ndl, p1, M1, p11(p11)(p2tog, p13) from next ndl. (23, 25, 27 heel sts on ndl)

Divide rem 23(25)(27) sts on 2 ndls and leave for later.

Work back and forth on heel sts only.

Row 1 (RS): sl 1, *k1, sl 1, rep from * across.

Row 2: Purl.

Rows 3–21(23)(25): Rep

Rows 1 and 2, ending with Row 1. (11, 12, 13 loops on each side of heel flap.)

Shape heel
Place safety pin marker in st #12(13)(14). Shaping takes place evenly spaced on each side of this center st.

Row 1 (WS): P14(15)(16), p2tog, p1, turn.

Row 2: sl 1, k6, k2tog, k1, turn.

Row 3: sl 1, p7, p2tog, p1, turn.

Row 4: sl 1, k8, k2tog, k1, turn.

Row 5: sl 1, p9, p2tog, p1, turn.

Row 6: sl 1, k10, k2tog, k1, turn.

Continue to work in this manner, having 1 more st before dec each row until all sts have been worked, ending with a RS row. For size M only, last WS row will end p2tog; turn, sl 1, k to last 2 sts, end k2tog. (15, 15, 17 heel sts rem)

Instep
Using ndl containing rem heel sts, pick up and k 11(12)(13) sts in loops along edge of heel flap (Ndl 1); with free ndl, k3(4)(5), pM, work in patt across 17 sts, pM, k3(4)(5) (23, 25, 27 instep sts on Ndl 2); pick up and k

11(12)(13) sts in loops along edge of heel flap, with same ndl, k7(7)(8) sts from Ndl 1 (18, 19, 21 sts on Ndl 3). (60, 64, 70 sts)

Rnd 1: K to marker, work 17 sts in est patt, k to end.

Rnd 2: K to last 3 sts on Ndl 1, k2tog, k1; work across Ndl 2 in est patt; at beg of Ndl 3, k1, ssk, k to end.

Rep Rnds 1 and 2 until a total of 23(25)(27) sts rem on Ndls 1 and 3, then work even in est patt until foot meas 7(8)(9)

inches or approximately 2 inches less than desired length. Cut MC, attach CC.

Toe

Rnd 1: Knit.

Rnd 2: K to last 3 sts on Ndl 1, k2tog, k1; on Ndl 2, k1, ssk, k to last 3 sts, k2tog, k1; on Ndl 3, k1, ssk, k to end.

Rep Rnds 1 and 2 until 22 sts rem (all sizes). With Ndl 3, k across sts from Ndl 1. (11 sts each on 2 ndls)

Weave toe

Cut yarn, leaving an 18-inch end. Thread yarn in tapestry ndl, hold ndls holding sts parallel, *insert ndl in first st on front ndl as if to purl, leave st on ndl, go into first st on back ndl as if to knit, sl st off ndl, go into next st on back ndl as if to purl, leave st on ndl, go into first st on front ndl as if to knit, sl st off ndl, rep from * until all sts have been worked. ❖

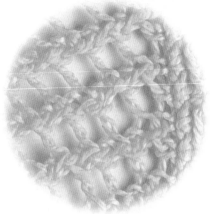

Garden Party Hat

Design by Diane Zangl

Worn first as a bridal accessory, after the ceremony it becomes delightful wall décor.

Experience Level
Intermediate***

Size
One size fits most

Finished Measurements
Head circumference: 21 inches

Brim depth: 6½ inches

Materials
- Patons Cotton DK 100 percent mercerized cotton (116 yds/50g per ball): 3 balls corn silk #6303
- Size 5 (3.75mm) double-pointed needles
- Size 6 (4mm) 16- and 24-inch circular needles or size needed to obtain gauge
- Size F/5 (3.75mm) crochet hook
- ⅔ yd (20-inch-wide) stiff buckram for interfacing
- ¼ yd (45-inch-wide) non-woven fabric for lining
- ⅔ yd (1-inch-wide) white grosgrain ribbon
- Liquid fabric stiffener
- Plastic bowl from whipped topping
- Flowers, ribbon or lace

Gauge
20 sts and 28 rnds = 4 inches/10cm with larger ndls in WSS patt

16 sts and 28 rnds = 4 inches/10cm with larger ndls in trellis lace patt

To save time, take time to check gauge.

Special Abbreviations
Wrap Slip St (WSS): Bring yarn to front, sl next st as if to p, take yarn to back.

Make 1 (M1): Make a backward lp and place it on RH ndl.

Pattern Stitches
A. Wrap Slip St Patt
Rnds 1, 2 and 3: Knit.

Rnd 4: *K5, WSS, rep from * around.

Rnds 5, 6 and 7: Knit.

Rnd 8: K2,*WSS, k5, rep from * around, ending with k3.

Rep Rnds 1–8 for patt.

B. Trellis Lace
Rnd 1: *Ssk, yo, rep from * around

Rnd 2: Knit.

Rep Rnds 1 and 2 for patt.

Hat
Top
With smaller dp ndls, CO 9 sts, leaving an 8-inch end for sewing opening. Join without twisting, pM between first and last sts. Knit 1 rnd.

Inc rnd: *K1, M1, rep from * around.

Knit 2 rnds. Rep inc rnd. Knit 4 rnds. Rep inc rnd. Knit 8 rnds.

Next inc rnd: *K3, M1, rep from * around. (96 sts)

Knit 2 rnds. Purl 1 rnd.

Sides
Change to larger 16-inch ndl. Work even in Patt A until side meas 3½ inches above purl rnd. BO, do not cut last lp. Drop yarn.

Brim
With RH ndl, pick up back lp only of each BO st. (96 sts)

Inc rnd: *K2, M1, k1, M1, rep from * around. (160 sts)

Work in Patt B until brim meas 6½ inches above picked up sts. BO very loosely in knit. Do not cut last lp. With crochet hook, work 2 sc in each BO st. Sl st to join.

Picot edge
*Ch 3, sl st in same st, sl st in next 4 sts, rep from * around. Fasten off.

Finishing
Cut 1 piece of interfacing 22 inches long x 3½ inches wide. Cut another piece of interfacing into a circle with a 6½-inch diameter. Sew one long side of rectangle around edge of circle, having a ¼-inch seam allowance. Overlap ends by ⅜ inch. Tack interfacing to inside top of

crown. Slipstitch edge of interfacing to crown ¼ inch above bottom edge.

Cut l piece of lining material 22 inches long x 4 inches wide. Cut another piece of lining into a circle with a 6 ½-inch diameter. With RS tog, sew short sides of rectangular piece tog with a ¼-inch seam. Sew one long edge of sidepiece to outer edge of circle. Pin lining to inside of crown along bottom edge, turning under ½ inch on raw edge. Slipstitch in place. Cut l piece of ribbon ½ inch longer than inside measurement of hat. Slipstitch in place over lining along bottom edge.

Stiffen hat brim only with fabric stiffener, following directions on package. Place hat over plastic bowl to hold shape of crown. Pin brim to a flat surface (a large piece of plastic foam works well), stretching and smoothing brim to open lace. Let dry thoroughly.

Trim as desired with ribbon, lace, flowers, etc. ❖

Mesh Hobo Bag

Design by Sue E. Hotovec

This oversized bag makes a great beach tote or an environmentally friendly shopping bag!

Experience Level
Intermediate***

Materials
- Aunt Lydia's Denim Quick Crochet Thread 75 percent cotton/25 percent acrylic (400 yds/8 oz per ball): 1 ball olive #1143
- Size 8 (5mm) double-pointed and 16-inch circular needles or size needed to obtain gauge
- Stitch markers
- Stitch holders
- Tapestry needle

Gauge
9 sts and 14½ rows = 4 inches/ 10cm in patt

Gauge is not critical in this project.

Special Abbreviation
Sdp: Sl next st to right ndl, drop yo, return sl st to left ndl, p2tog.

Pattern Note
Inc by knitting in front and back of st.

After working a rnd that drops yo's, pull down on work to get yarn loops out of the way for next rnd.

Using dpn CO 8 sts and join without twisting. Mark beg of rnd.

Rnds 1, 3, 5, 7 and 9: Knit.

Rnd 2: Inc 1 in each st around. (16 sts)

Rnd 4: *K1, inc 1, rep from * around. (24 sts)

Rnd 6: *K2, inc 1, rep from * around. (32 sts)

Rnd 8: *K3, inc 1, rep from * around. (40 sts)

Rnd 10: *K4, inc 1, rep from * around. (48 sts)

Rnd 11: Knit.

Change to **Rnd 1:** [*K1, yo, rep from * to 1 st before marker, {k1, yo, k1b} in last st] 8 times.

Rnd 2: K the knit sts, dropping yo's.

Rep Rnds 1 and 2 until there are 17 sts in each section after Rnd 2. (136 sts total)

Continue to work even in patt, working [k1, yo] around on Rnd 1 and Rnd 2 as above until piece meas 15 inches from beg, ending with Rnd 2.

Divide for shoulder straps
BO 4 sts, [k1, yo] to 4th marker, turn, leaving rem sts for later.

Next row: Purl back, dropping yo's. (64 sts)

Row 1: K2tog, yo, *k1, yo, rep from * to last 2 sts, k2tog.

Row 2: Sdp, purl back dropping yo's to last 3 sts, sdp.

Rep Rows 1 and 2 until 20 sts rem after Row 2.

*Next row: [K1, yo] across. Rep Row 2 above. Rep from * until 10 sts rem.

Shoulder strap
Row 1: *K1, yo, rep from * across. (20 sts)

Row 2: Purl across.

Beg double knit section
Use 3 dpn.

Row 1 (RS ndl): *K1, yo, sl 1 st to second dpn, rep from * across. (20 sts on RS dpn, 10 sts on WS dpn)

Row 1 (WS ndl): *K1, yo, rep from * across ndl. (20 sts on each ndl)

Row 2: *K1, drop yo, rep from * across each ndl. (10 sts on each ndl)

Row 3: *K1, yo, rep from * across each ndl. (20 sts on each ndl)

[Rep Rows 2 and 3] 8 times or until strap is desired length, ending with Row 2. Keep in mind that bag and strap will stretch with use.

Place sts from each ndl on separate holder and cut yarn, leaving a 12-inch end.

Complete other side as above.

Finishing
Weave outside sts of strap ends tog, then turn work over and weave inside sts. ❖

Seed & Cables Ski Tam

Design by Helen Stenborg

Be right in style with this quick-to-knit tam made of bulky weight acrylic yarn. Match your favorite ski sweater.

Experience Level
Intermediate***

Size
Woman's: one size fits most

Materials
- Lion Brand Jiffy bulky weight acrylic yarn (135 yds/3 oz per ball): 1 ball fisherman #099
- Size 6 (4mm) 16-inch circular needle
- Size 8 (5mm) double-pointed and 16-inch circular needles or size needed to obtain gauge
- Stitch markers
- Cable needle
- Tapestry needle

Gauge
12 sts and 20 rnds = 4 inches/10cm in seed st with larger ndls

To save time, take time to check gauge.

Special Abbreviation
Back cross (BC): Sl next 3 sts to cn, hold in back, k3, k3 from cn.

Pattern Stitch
Seed St (on even number of sts)

Rnd 1: *K1, p1, rep from * around.

Rnd 2: *P1, k1, rep from * around.

Rep Rnds 1 and 2 for patt.

With smaller circular ndl, CO 80 sts. Join without twisting, mark beg of rnd and work in k1, p1 ribbing for 2 inches. Change to larger circular ndl.

Beg patt
Rnds 1–9: [Work seed st across 10 sts, k6] 5 times.

Rnd 10: [Work seed st across 10 sts, BC] 5 times.

Rep Rnds 1–10 until piece meas 6 inches from beg.

Shape top
Change to dpn, pM every 16 sts (5 sections) and work in St st.

Rnd 1: [K1, k2tog, k to within 3 sts of next marker, ssk, k1] 5 times.

A Berry Special Scarf

Continued from page 52

k9, p3.

Row 8: P3, [k3, sl2togk, k1, p2sso, k3, p5] 8 times, k3, sl2togk, k1, p2sso, k3, p3. (109 sts)

Rows 9 and 11: K3, [p7, k5] 8 times, p7, k3.

Row 10: P3, [k7, p5] 8 times, k7, p3.

Row 12: P3, [k2, sl2togk, k1, p2sso, k2, p5] 8 times, k2, sl2togk, k1, p2sso, k2, p3. (91 sts)

Rows 13 and 15: K3, [p5, k5] 8 times, p5, k3.

Row 14: P3, [k5, p5] 8 times, k5, p3.

Row 16: P3, [k1, sl2togk, k1, p2sso, k1, p5] 8 times, k1, sl2togk, k1, p2sso, k1, p3. (73 sts)

Rows 17 and 19: K3, [p3, k5] 8 times, p3, k3.

Row 18: P3, [k3, p5] 8 times, k3, p3.

Row 20: P3, [sl2togk, k1, p2sso, p5] 8 times, sl2togk, k1, p2sso, p3. (55 sts)

Row 21: K1, M1, k2 [p1, k5] 8 times, p1, k2, M1, k1. (57 sts)

Continue in berry patt for body of scarf.

Berry Patt

Row 1 (RS): K1, p3, [k1, p5] 8 times, k1, p3, k1.

Row 2: P1, k3tog, [yo, {k1, yo, k1} in next st, k5tog] 8 times, yo, {k1, yo, k1} in next st, yo, k3tog, p1.

Rows 3 and 5: K2 [p5, k1] 9 times, k1.

Row 4: P2, [k5, p1] 9 times, p1.

Row 6: P1, k2 in next st, [yo, k5tog, yo, {k1, yo, k1} in next st] 8 times, yo, k5tog, yo, k2 in next st, p1.

Row 7: Rep Row 1.

Row 8: P1, k3, [p1, k5] 8 times, p1, k3, p1.

Rep Rows 1–8 until piece meas 23 inches from CO edge, ending with Row 4. Leave sts on holder or spare ndl.

Rep for second half of scarf. Weave halves tog at center back.

Wash gently in mild soap or wool wash, lay flat to dry. ❖

Rnd 2: Knit.

Rep Rnds 1 and 2 until 20 sts rem, then k2tog around.

Divide sts evenly on 2 ndls and weave tog.

Top knot

With larger ndls, CO 28 sts and work in k2, p2 for 12 rows. Cut yarn, leaving an 18-inch end.

Thread end in tapestry ndl and run through rem sts, draw up tightly. With same end, seam edges of piece tog, run end through CO sts, pull tight and fasten off. Sew to top of tam. Block lightly. ❖

Pretty Petals Collars

Continued from page 69

Row 13: K1, [k1, k2tog, yo] 3 times, k2tog, p2tog, ssk, [yo, ssk, k1] 3 times, k1.

Row 15: K1, p9, p3tog, p9, k1. (21 sts)

Sl first 10 sts to separate ndl, fold in half with RS together and BO as follows: hold ndls containing sts parallel, with 3rd ndl, k first st on front ndl and first 2 sts on back ndl tog, *k next st on both ndls tog, BO 1, rep from * until all sts are worked, fasten off.

Press petal through a damp cloth to flatten it out.

Finishing
Join petals

Refer to Fig.1, beg at center back, place 1 petal over another, overlapping halfway. Place third petal over bottom petal on other side, again overlapping halfway. First (bottom) petal is center back. Place a 4th petal over 3rd, again overlapping halfway. Continue in this fashion on each side until 4 overlapping petals are on each side of center back. Pin or baste in place.

Neck band

With RS facing, beg at right center front, pick up and k 110 sts across entire top edge of overlapped petals. Pull sts up through both layers where petals overlap. Turn and k 1 row, then work 8 rows St st. BO all sts.

Fold band to inside and sew in place. Cut yarn, leaving a long tail.

Button loop

With crochet hook, pull up a loop next to long tail left after sewing band. Work 11 sc around tail. Fold in half and sew in place to form a loop. Sew button to other side of collar. ❖

Fig. 1

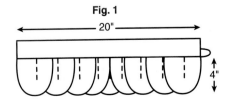

Row 18: *K7, yo, sl 1, k2tog, psso, yo, k7, rep from * across.

Row 20: K1, *yo, k2tog, rep from * across.

Rows 21 and 22: Knit.

For 14-inch piece of lace, CO 119 sts and work Rows 1–22 of patt. BO all sts knitwise. ❖

Baby Soft Blanket Edging

Experience Level
Intermediate***

Finished Size
Approximately 2¼ inches wide x 1¼ inches per rep

Materials
- Sesia Baby sport weight cotton yarn (196 yds/ 50g per ball): 1 ball blue #71
- Size 3 (3.25mm) needles or size needed to obtain gauge

Gauge
7 sts = 1 inch/2.5cm in patt

To save time, take time to check gauge.

CO 16 sts.

Row 1 (RS): K3, [yo, p1, p3tog, p1, yo, k1] twice, [k1, p1, k1] in last st. (18 sts)

Rows 2, 4, 6 and 8: [P2tog] twice, pass first st over second st, yo, p14. (16 sts)

Row 3: K4, yo, sl 1, k2tog, psso, yo, k3, yo, sl 1, k2tog, psso, yo, k2, [k1, p1, k1] in last st. (18 sts)

Row 5: K2, p2tog, p1, yo, k1, yo, p1, p3tog, p1, yo, k1, yo, p1, p2tog, [k1, p1, k1] in last st. (18 sts)

Row 7: K2, k2tog, yo, k3, yo, sl 1, k2tog, psso, yo, k3, yo, ssk, [k1, p1, k1] in last st. (18 sts)

Rep Rows 1–8 for desired length. BO all sts. ❖

Plumes Lace

Experience Level
Intermediate***

Finished Size
Approximately 2½ inches wide x ⅝ inch per rep

Materials
- Grignasco Cotton 5 mercerized cotton (200 yds/50g per ball): 1 ball white #001
- Size 2 (2.75mm) needles or size needed to obtain gauge

Gauge
11 sts and 12 rows = 2 inches/ 5cm in patt

To save time, take time to check gauge.

CO 9 sts. Knit 1 row.

Row 1 (RS): K1, yo, p2tog, [k1, p1, k1] in next st, k15. (21 sts)

Row 2: P15, k3, yo, p2tog, k1. (21 sts)

Row 3: K1, yo, p2tog, k3, [k2tog] twice, pass first st over second st, [yo, k1] 5 times, yo, [k2tog] twice, pass first st over second st, k2. (21 sts)

Row 4: P15, [k1, BO 1 st] twice, [yo, p1] twice, [k1, BO 1 st] twice. (19 sts)

Rep Rows 1–4 for desired length. BO all sts. ❖

The Finishing Touch

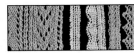

Continued from page 61

Gauge

5 sts = 1 inch/2.5cm in patt

To save time, take time to check gauge.

CO 18 sts.

Row 1 (RS): K1, yo, k2tog, k3, yo, ssk, k2, k2tog, yo, k1, yo, ssk, yo, k3. (19 sts)

Rows 2 and 4: Purl.

Row 3: K1, yo, k2tog, k1, k2tog, yo, k1, yo, ssk, k1, k2tog, yo, k1, yo, ssk, yo, k4. (20 sts)

Row 5: K1, yo, [k2tog] twice, yo, k3, yo, ssk, k2tog, yo, k1, yo, ssk, yo, k5. (21 sts)

Row 6: BO 3 sts purlwise, p to end. (18 sts)

Rep Rows 1–6 for desired length. BO all sts.

Trailing Vines Lace

Experience Level
Advanced Beginner**

Finished Size
Approximately ¾ inch wide x ⁵⁄₁₆ inch per rep

Materials
- Coats Opera #20 crochet cotton (445 yds/50g per ball): 1 ball mauve #582
- Size 0 (2mm) needles or size needed to obtain gauge

Gauge
10 sts = 1 inch/2.5cm in patt

To save time, take time to check gauge.

CO 8 sts

Row 1 (RS): K2, yo, k3, yo, k1, yo, k2tog. (10 sts)

Row 2: Yo, p2tog, p6, k2. (10 sts)

Row 3: K3, sl 1, k2tog, psso, k2, yo, k2tog. (8 sts)

Row 4: Yo, p2tog, p4, k2. (8 sts)

Rep Rows 1–4 for desired length. BO all sts. ❖

Slip-Stitch Mittens, Scarf & Ski Band

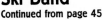

Continued from page 45

beg. Place 14 gusset sts (7 on each side of marker) on holder or scrap yarn, CO 5 sts above thumb hole on next rnd (51 sts) and continue to work in patt until mitten meas 11½ inches from beg. Cut B and complete mitten with A.

Shape tip

Rnd 1: *K1, p1, rep from * around.

Rnd 2: P1, *k2tog, p1, k1, p1, rep from * around.

Rep Rnds 1 and 2 until 6 sts rem. Thread yarn through these sts and fasten off securely.

Thumb

With A, work across sts from holder, pick up and k 1 st in corner, 5 sts across CO sts, 1 st in corner. (21 sts)

Working in St st, work 1 inch in A, ½ inch in B, ½ inch in A. Change to B, k 1 rnd, then k2tog around until 4 sts rem. Pull yarn through these sts and fasten off securely. ❖

Ski Band

Experience Level
Intermediate***

Finished Measurements
Approximately 3 x 20 inches

Materials
- Yarn by Mills washable merino wool worsted weight yarn (130 yds/2 oz per skein): 1 skein each variegated (A), solid color (B)
- Size 5 (3.75mm) 16-inch circular needle
- Tapestry needle

Gauge

28 sts = 4 inches/10cm in patt

To save time, take time to check gauge.

With B, CO 138 sts, pM at beg of rnd and join without twisting. Work in k1, p1 ribbing for 3 rnds.

Beg patt

Rnds 1 and 2: With B, knit.

Rnds 3 and 4: With A, *k2, sl 1, rep from * around.

Rep Rnds 1–4 until piece meas 2¾ inches, ending with Rnd 2. Cut A.

With B, work in k1, p1 ribbing for 3 rnds. BO all sts in rib.

Block lightly. ❖

Kidstuff To Go

*K*nitting for kids is fun and easy with these colorful and creative projects. Take those moments when you're waiting for your children to finish sport practices, watching them at a dance rehearsal or attending one of their events to knit these on-the-go projects. Before long your project will be complete and ready to give to your precious child.

Chapter 3

Peas in a Pod Cardigan

Design by E. J. Slayton

*Knit this beautifully constructed cardigan
for your precious little one.*

Experience Level
Intermediate***

Size
Child's 2(4)(6)(8)(10)
Instructions are given for
smallest size, with larger
sizes in parentheses. When
only 1 number is given, it
applies to all sizes.

Finished Measurements
Chest: 21(23)(25)(27)(30)
inches
Length: 11½(14)(15½)(17)
(20½) inches

Sleeve underarm:
9¼(10½)(12½)(14)(16) inches

Materials
- Falk 100 percent super-
  wash wool worsted
  weight yarn from Dale
  of Norway (116 yds/50g
  per ball): 4(5)(6)(7)(9)
  skeins green #8426
- Size 4 (3.5mm) 24-inch
  circular needle
- Size 6 (4mm) needles or
  size needed to obtain
  gauge
- Stitch markers
- Stitch holders
- Cable needle
- Tapestry needle
- 5(5)(5)(6)(6) ½-inch buttons #90655 from JHB
  International Inc.

Gauge
20 sts and 28 rows = 4 inches/
10cm in Patt A with larger ndls

To save time, take time to
check gauge.

Special Abbreviations
Make 1 (M1): Inc by making
a backward loop over right ndl.

**Central Double Decrease
(cdd):** Sl next 2 sts as if to
k2tog, k1, p2sso.

Pattern Stitches
A. Diamond Net (multiple
of 8 sts + 1)

Row 1 (RS): K4, *p1, k7,
rep from * across, end p1, k4

Row 2: P3, *k1, p1, k1, p5,
rep from * across, end k1, p1,
k1, p3.

Row 3: K2, *p1, k3, rep
from * across, end p1, k2.

Row 4: *P1, k1, p5, k1, rep
from * across, end p1.

Row 5: P1, *k7, p1, rep
from * across.

Row 6: Rep Row 4.

Row 7: Rep Row 3.

Row 8: Rep Row 2.
Rep Rows 1–8 for patt.

B. Back Cable with Knot
(panel of 7 sts)

Row 1 (RS): P1, sl next 3
sts to cn, hold in back, k2, k3
from cn, p1.

Rows 2, 4, and 6: K1, p5, k1.
Rows 3 and 7: P1, k5, p1.

Row 5: P1, k2, in next st
[k1, {p1, k1} twice, pass first 4
sts over last st], k2, p1.

Row 8: Rep Row 2.
Rep Rows 1–8 for patt.

C. Front Cable with Knot
(panel of 7 sts)

Row 1 (RS): P1, sl next 2
sts to cn, hold in front, k3, k2
from cn, p1.

Rows 2–8: Work as cable B.
Rep Rows 1–8 for patt.

Back
With smaller ndls, CO 54(58)
(66)(70)(78) sts.

Row 1 (WS): P2, *k2, p2,
rep from * across.

Row 2: K2, *p2, k2, rep
from * across.

Rep Rows 1 and 2 until piece
meas 1½(1½)(2)(2)(2) inches
from beg, ending with Row 2.

Next row: Purl, inc 7(7)(5)
(5)(5) sts evenly across. (61,
65, 71, 75, 83 sts)

Beg patt
Change to larger ndl and
work patt from Chart A, beg
and ending as indicated for
size and keeping 2 selvage sts
in St st throughout, until
piece meas 6½(8½)(9½)(10½)
(13½) inches from beg ending
with a WS row.

Shape armholes
At beg of next 2 rows, BO
4(4)(6)(6)(8) sts, then dec 1 st

each side [every RS row] 5 times. (43, 47, 51, 55, 57 sts rem)

Work even in est patt until piece meas 11½(14)(15½)(17) (20½) inches from beg. Mark center 23(23)(25)(25)(27) sts for back neck, sl all sts to holder.

Left Front

With smaller ndl, CO 30(30) (34)(34)(38) sts and work ribbing as for back, ending with Row 2.

Next row: P2, pM, k1, M1, [k1, M1] twice, pM, p to end, inc 0(2)(1)(3)(3) sts evenly across. (33, 35, 38, 40, 44 sts)

Beg patt

Change to larger ndl.

Row 1 (RS): K2 (selvage sts), work patt A from Chart A across 21(23)(26)(28)(32) sts, beg as indicated for size, k1, sl M, work Row 1 of patt B across 7 sts, sl M, end k2 (selvage sts).

Work in est patts until front meas same as back to underarm, ending with a WS row.

Shape armhole

At beg of next row BO 4(4)(6)(6)(8) sts, then dec 1 st at armhole edge [every RS row] 5 times. (24, 26, 27, 29, 31 sts rem)

Continue to work even until piece meas 9(11½)(12½) (14)(17½) inches from beg, ending with a WS row.

Shape neck

Work in patt to last 11(11)(11) (11)(13) sts, sl these sts to a holder, and work on rem sts, dec 1 st at neck edge [eor] 3 times, then work even until front meas same as back to shoulder. Sl rem 10(12)(13) (15)(15) shoulder sts to a holder.

Right Front

Work as for left front, using patt C instead of B, reversing

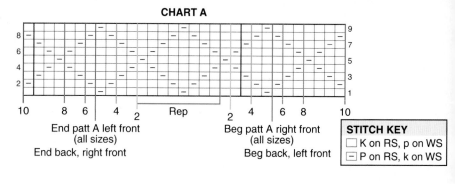

CHART A

End patt A left front (all sizes)
End back, right front

Rep

Beg patt A right front (all sizes)
Beg back, left front

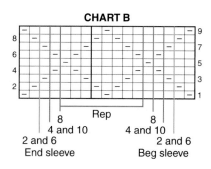

CHART B

Rep

8
4 and 10
2 and 6
End sleeve

8
4 and 10
2 and 6
Beg sleeve

patt placement and shaping. Seam shoulders.

Sleeves

With smaller ndl, CO 26(34)(34) (38)(42) sts and work ribbing as for back, ending with Row 2.

Next row: Purl, inc 7(5)(7) (7)(5) sts evenly across. (33, 39, 41, 45, 47 sts)

Change to larger ndl and beg patt from Chart B, beg and ending as indicated for size and keeping 2 selvage sts in St st throughout.

At the same time, inc 1 st at each edge [every 4th row] 4 times, then [every 6th row] 5(4)(6)(6)(8) times. (51, 55, 61, 65, 71 sts)

Work even in patt until sleeve meas 9¼(10½)(12½)(14)(16) inches or desired length to underarm, ending with a WS row.

Shape sleeve cap

At beg of next 2 rows, BO 4(4)(6)(6)(8) sts, then dec 1 st each side [every RS row] 5 times. BO knitwise from WS.

Finishing

Front border

With smaller circular ndl and RS facing, beg at bottom of right front, pick up and k 2 sts for every 3 rows to neck edge, pM, M1, k across front neck sts from holder, dec 3 sts across top of cable, pM, pick up and k14(14)(16)(16)(16) sts along right front neck edge, k across back neck sts, work left front to match right side.

Note: *For ease in working shaping, replace markers with a safety pin placed in each corner st.*

Row 1 (WS): Sl 1, k to end.

Row 2: Sl 1, k to first marked st, M1, k1, M1, [k to 1 st before next marked st, work cdd] twice, k to last marked st, M1, k1, M1, k to end.

Row 3: Rep Row 1, working 5(5)(5)(6)(6) buttonholes [k2tog, yo, ssk] in right front band, placing top hole right at the corner, bottom hole 3 or 4 sts from bottom and rem holes evenly spaced bet.

Row 4: Work as Row 2, working [k1, p1] in each yo across.

Rows 5 and 6: Rep Rows 1 and 2.

BO all sts knitwise from WS.

Set sleeves into armholes. Sew sleeve and body underarm seams.

Sew buttons on left band opposite buttonholes. Block lightly. ❖

Diamonds & Braids Gansey

Design by E. J. Slayton

Your child will enjoy the warmth and comfort of a multiseasonal gansey.

Experience Level
Intermediate***

Size
Child's 4(6)(8)(10)
Instructions are given for smallest size, with larger sizes in parentheses. When only 1 number is given, it applies to all sizes.

Finished Measurements
Chest: 23(25)(27)(30) inches
Length: 14(15½)(17)(20½) inches
Sleeve length: 10½(12½) (14)(16) inches

Materials
• Brown Sheep Co. Cotton Fleece 80 percent pima cotton/20 percent merino wool worsted weight yarn (215 yds/100g per skein): 3(3)(4)(5) skeins lapis #CW-590
• Size 4 (3.5mm) straight and 16-inch circular needles
• Size 6 (4mm) needles or size needed to obtain gauge
• Cable needle
• Stitch markers
• Stitch holders
• Tapestry needle

Gauge
20 sts and 28 rows = 4 inches/ 10cm in diamond patt with larger ndls

To save time, take time to check gauge.

Special Abbreviations
Back Cross (BC): Sl next 2 sts to cn, hold in back, k2, k2 from cn.

Front Cross (FC): Sl next 2 sts to cn, hold in front, k2, k2 from cn.

Make 1 (M1): Inc by making a backward loop over right ndl.

Pattern Stitches
A. Diamonds (multiple of 9 sts + 2)

Row 1 (RS): P2, *k3, p1, k3, p2, rep from * across.

Row 2: K2, *p3, k1, p3, k2, rep from * across.

Row 3: P2, *k2, p1, k1, p1, k2, p2, rep from * across.

Row 4: K2, *p2, k1, p1, k1, p2, k2, rep from * across.

Row 5: P2, *k3, p1, k3, p2, rep from * across.

Row 6: K2, *p3, k1, p3, k2, rep from * across.

Row 7: P2, *k7, p2, rep from * across.

Row 8: K2, *p7, k2, rep from * across.

Rep Rows 1–8 for patt.

B. Aran Braid Cables
(panel of 18 sts)

Row 1 (RS): P2, k2, FC, p2, BC, k2, p2.

Rows 2 and 4: K2, [p6, k2] twice.

Row 3: P2, BC, k2, p2, k2, FC, p2.

Rep Rows 1–4 for patt.

Back
With smaller ndls CO 62(66)(74)(78) sts.

Row 1 (WS): P2, *k2, p2, rep from * across.

Row 2: K2, *p2, k2, rep from * across.

Rep Rows 1 and 2 until ribbing meas 1½(2)(2)(2) inches from beg, ending with a WS row.

Next row: Knit, inc 6(8)(6)(8) sts evenly across. (68, 74, 80, 86 sts)

Work in St st for 8(10)(10) (12) rows.

Knit 3 rows. (2 ridges of garter st)

Set up patt
Next row (RS): K1 (selvage st), pM, p1(0)(0)(1), k7(2)(5)(7), [p2, k7] 2(3)(3)(3) times, pM, p2, [M1, k1] twice, k2, p2, k2, [k1, M1] twice, p2, pM, [k7, p2] 2(3)(3)(3) times, k7(2)(5)(7), p1(0)(0)(1), pM, k1 (selvage st). (72, 78, 84, 90 sts)

Next row: P1, k1(0)(0)(1),

CHART A

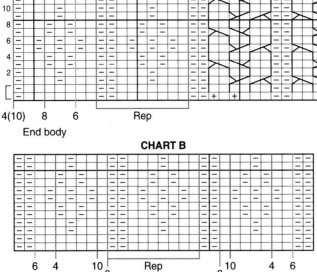

4(10) 8 6 Rep · Rep 6 8 4(10)

End body · Beg body

CHART B

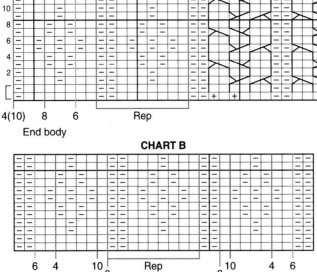

6 4 10 Rep 10 4 6
8 · 8

End sleeve · Beg sleeve

STITCH KEY

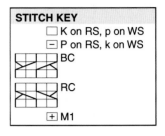

☐ K on RS, p on WS
⊟ P on RS, k on WS
◹ BC
◹ RC
⊞ M1

p7(2)(5)(7), [k2, p7] 2(3)(3)(3) times, k2, [p6, k2] twice, [p7, k2]2(3)(3)(3) times, p7(2)(5) (7), k1(0)(0)(1), p1.

Beg patt

Beg and ending as indicated and keeping 1 selvage st at each edge in St st throughout, work in patt from Chart A until piece meas 8½(9½)(10½) (13½) inches from beg, ending with a WS row.

Shape underarms

Maintaining est patt, at beg of next 2 rows, BO 4(5)(6)(7) sts, then dec 1 st at each side [eor] 5 times. (54, 58, 62, 66 sts)

Work even until armhole meas 5½(6)(6½)(7) inches, ending with a WS row. Mark center 32(32)(34)(36) sts for neck, place all sts on holder.

Front

Work as for back until armhole meas 3(3)(3½)(4) inches, ending with a WS row.

Shape neck

Work 15(17)(18)(19) sts in est patt, place center 24(24)(26) (28) sts on holder, join 2nd ball of yarn and complete row.

Continuing to work both

sides at once with separate balls of yarn, dec 1 st at each neck edge [eor] 4 times. (11, 13, 14, 15 sts rem for each shoulder)

Work even until front meas same as back at shoulder.

BO front and back shoulder sts tog as follows:

Hold ndls containing shoulder sts parallel, right sides tog; with 3rd ndl, k first st on front and back ndls tog, *k next st on both ndls tog, BO 1, rep from * until all sts are worked, fasten off. Rep for 2nd shoulder.

Sleeves

With smaller ndls, CO 34(38) (42)(42) sts and work in ribbing as for back until ribbing meas 1½(2)(2)(2) inches from beg, ending with a WS row.

Next row: Knit, inc 7(7)(7) (9) sts evenly across. (41, 45, 49, 51 sts)

Keeping 2 sts at each edge in St st throughout, knit 3 rows (2 ridges), inc 1 st at each side on next RS row. (43, 47, 51, 53 sts)

Set up patt

Beg and ending as indicated, work in patt from Chart B, inc 1

st each side [every 8th row] 7(7) (8)(10) times. (59, 63, 69, 75 sts)

Continue to work even in est patt until sleeve meas 10½(12½) (14)(16) inches or desired length to underarm, ending with a WS row.

Shape cap

At beg of next 2 rows, BO 4(5)(6)(7) sts, then dec 1 st at each side [eor] 5 times. On last WS row, BO all sts knitwise.

Finishing
Neck band

With smaller 16-inch circular ndl, pick up and k 12(14)(14) (14) sts along left neck edge, work front neck sts from holder, dec 2 sts across top of each cable, pick up and k 12(14) (14)(14) sts along right neck edge, work back neck sts from holder, dec 2 sts across top of each cable. (72, 76, 80, 84 sts)

Purl 1 rnd, then work in k2, p2 ribbing, centering patt at front neck, until ribbing meas 2 inches. Do not BO.

Fold ribbing to inside and sew loosely to beg of ribbing.

Set sleeves into armholes. Sew sleeve and body underarms. Block lightly. ❖

Baby Cables Bootie Socks

Design by Dawn Brocco

Knit up these cute socks with simple cables.
They can be worn any season of the year.

Experience Level

Intermediate***

Size

Infant's size 3(6)(12) months Instructions are given for smallest size, with larger sizes in parentheses. When only 1 number is given, it applies to all sizes.

Finished Measurements

Circumference: 4(4½)(5) inches

Foot length: 3¾(4¼)(4¾) inches

Heel to top of cuff: 3¾ (3¾)(4½) inches

Materials

- Naturally Magic Garden Cotton Candy Baby DK 70 percent cotton/30 percent wool DK weight yarn (115 yds/50g per skein): 1 skein sherbert #503
- Size 2 (2.75mm) double-pointed needles or size needed to obtain gauge
- Tapestry needle

Gauge

7 sts and 10 rows = 1 inch/2.5 cm in St st.

To save time, take time to check gauge.

Pattern Stitch

Baby Cable Ribbing

Rnds 1, 2 and 4: *K2, p2, rep from * around.

Rnd 3: *K1 in 2nd st on LH ndl, k1 in first st, sl both sts off tog, p2, rep from * around.

Rep Rnds 1–4 for patt.

Sock

CO 32(36)(40) sts, divide on 3 ndls. Mark beg of rnd and work in rib patt for 16(16)(20) rnds.

Heel flap

K next 16(18)(20) sts. Work in St st on these 16(18)(20) sts for 15(17)(19) more rows, ending on a WS row.

Shape heel

Size 3 mos: K8, ssk, k1, turn. Sl 1, p1, p2tog, p1, turn. Sl 1, k2, ssk, k1, turn. Sl 1, p3, p2tog, p1, turn. Sl 1, k4, ssk, k1, turn. Sl 1, p5, p2tog, p1, turn. Sl 1, k6, ssk, turn. Sl 1, p6, p2tog, turn. (8 sts rem)

Size 6 mos: K9, ssk, k1, turn. Sl 1, p1, p2tog, p1, turn. Sl 1, k2, ssk, k1, turn. Sl 1, p3, p2tog, p1, turn. Sl 1, k4, ssk, k1, turn. Sl 1, p5, p2tog, p1, turn. Sl 1, k6, ssk, k1, turn. Sl 1, p7, p2tog, p1, turn. (10 sts rem)

Size 12 mos: K10, ssk, k1, turn. Sl 1, p1, p2tog, p1, turn. Sl 1, k2, ssk, k1, turn. Sl 1, p3, p2tog, p1, turn. Sl 1, k4, ssk, k1, turn. Sl 1, p5, p2tog, p1, turn. Sl 1, k6, ssk, k1, turn. Sl 1, p7, p2tog, p1, turn. Sl 1, k8, ssk, turn. Sl 1, p8, p2tog, turn. (10 sts rem)

All sizes: Sl 1, k7(9)(9), with same ndl, pick up and k 8(9)(10) sts along right edge of heel flap; continue est cable rib patt across next 16(18)(20) sts, beg with Rnd 1 of patt; with separate ndl, pick up and k 8(9)(10) sts along left edge of heel flap, with same ndl, k 4(5)(5) heel sts. Rnds now begin at center heel.

Shape instep

Rnd 1: Knit.

Rnd 2: K to last 3 sts on first ndl, ssk, k1; continue cable rib patt across next 16(18)(20) sts; at beg of last ndl, k1, k2tog, k to end.

Rep Rnds 1 and 2 until 16(18)(20) sts rem on first and last ndls tog. (32, 36, 40 sts total)

Foot

Continue in est patts (St st for bottom and cable rib for top), until 20(24)(28) rnds of cable rib patt are completed, counting from beg of instep shaping.

Shape toe

For size 3 mos 12 mos

Rnd 1: *K6, k2tog, rep from * around.

Rnds 2, 4, 6, 8 and 10:
Knit.

Rnd 3: *K5, k2tog, rep from * around.

Rnd 5: *K4, k2tog, rep from * around.

Rnd 7: *K3, k2tog, rep from * around.

Rnd 9: *K2, k2tog, rep from * around.

Rnd 11: *K1, k2tog, rep from * around.

Rnd 12: [K2tog] around. (4, 5 sts rem)

For size 6 mos

Work Rnds 5–12 above. (6 sts rem)

Break yarn. With tapestry ndl, pull through rem sts and fasten off. ❖

Fun With Fibonacci!

Design by E. J. Slayton

The stripes may be based on a mathematical sequence, but the fun comes when you are knitting or wearing them!

Experience Level
Intermediate***

Size
Kid's extra small(small) (medium) (large) Instructions are given for smallest size, with larger sizes in parentheses. When only 1 number is given, it applies to all sizes.

Finished Measurements
Top: 4¾(5½)(6½)(6½) inches
Foot length: 5½(6½)(7½) (8½) inches

Materials
• Froelich Wolle Aurora 100 percent wool worsted weight yarn (105 yds/50g per skein): 1(2)(2)(2) skeins each medium blue #8343 (A), red #8352 (B), 1 skein royal blue #8317 (C), small amount white #8320 (D)
• Size 4 (3.5mm) double-pointed needles or size needed to obtain gauge
• Heel and toe reinforcement or Wooly Nylon (optional)
• Safety pin
• Tapestry needle

Gauge
12 sts and 14 rnds = 2 inches/ 5cm in St st

To save time, take time to check gauge.

Pattern Notes
Stripe patt is based on the Fibonacci series in which the next number is the sum of the 2 numbers before it. Beginning with 1, 1 + 1 = 2, 1 + 2 = 3, 2 + 3 = 5, 3 + 5 = 8 and so on as far as you want to go. Except for the ribbing (13 rnds), this sock uses stripes 1 through 8 rnds wide, but it would be interesting to try some of the larger numbers on a sweater or afghan. Varying the number of steps in the sequence and the number of colors can also give interesting results.

Stripe sequence
Ribbing, 13 rnds A; 1 rnd B, 2 rnds C, 3 rnds D, 5 rnds C, 8 rnds B, 5 rnds A (end xs, approximately 4¾ inches), 3 rnds B, 2 rnds C, 1 rnd D, 2 rnds C (end s, approximately 5½ inches), 3 rnds B, 5 rnds A (end m/l, approximately 6½ inches).

Sock
With A, CO 32(36)(40)(44) sts. Join, being careful not to twist and work in k2, p2 ribbing for 13 rnds.

Work in St st and stripe sequence until top meas 4¾ (5½)(6½)(6½) inches or desired length from beg.

Heel
With B, k next 8(9)(10)(12) sts for heel, turn and sl last 8(9) (10)(12) sts of previous rnd onto same ndl; divide rem 16(18)(20)(22) sts bet 2 ndls for instep to be worked later.

Working in rows on heel sts only, p across.

Row 1 (RS): *Sl 1, k1, rep from * across.

Row 2: Sl 1, purl across.

Rows 3–15(17)(19)(21): Rep Rows 1 and 2, ending with Row 1. (8, 9, 10, 11 sl st loops on each side of heel flap)

Shape heel
Place safety pin bet st #8(9)(10)(11) and next st. Shaping takes place evenly spaced on each side of marker.

Row 1 (WS): P10(11)(12)(13), p2tog, turn.

Row 2: Sl 1, k6, k2tog, k1, turn.

Row 3: Sl 1, p7, p2tog, p1, turn.

Row 4: Sl 1, k8, k2tog, k1, turn.

Row 5: Sl 1, p9, p2tog, p1, turn.

Continue to work in this manner, having 1 more st before dec each row until all sts have been worked, ending with a RS row. (10, 12, 12, 14 heel sts rem)

Instep
With B and ndl containing

rem heel sts, pick up and k 8(9)(10)(11) sts along edge of heel flap (Ndl 1); k16(18)(20)(22) instep sts (Ndl 2); with free ndl, pick up and k 8(9)(10)(11) sts along left edge of heel flap, k5(6)(6)(7) heel sts from Ndl 1 (Ndl 3). (42, 48, 52, 58 sts total)

Rnd 1: Knit.

Rnd 2: K to 3 sts from end of Ndl 1, k2tog, k1; k across Ndl 2; on Ndl 3, k1, ssk, k to end.

Change to B and rep Rnds 1 and 2 until a total of 16(18)(20)(22) sts rem on Ndls 1 and 3. (32, 36, 40, 44 sts rem)

Work even with B until foot meas 4(5½)(6½)(7½) inches, or approximately 1½ inches less than desired length.

Note: *To work stripes as shown, when foot meas approximately 2½ inches less than desired length, work 3 rnds B, 2 rnds C, 1 rnd B, then complete toe with C.*

Toe

Rnd 1: Knit.

Rnd 2: K to 3 sts from end of Ndl 1, k2tog, k1; on Ndl 2, k1, ssk, k to 3 sts from end, k2tog, k1; on Ndl 3, k1, ssk, k to end.

Rep Rnds 1 and 2 until

16(16)(20)(20) sts rem. With Ndl 3, work across sts from Ndl 1. (8, 8, 10, 10 sts each on 2 ndls)

Weave toe

Cut yarn, leaving an 18-inch end. Thread yarn in tapestry ndl, hold ndls holding sts parallel, *insert ndl in first st on front ndl as if to purl, leave st on ndl, go into first st on back ndl as if to knit, sl st off ndl, go into next st on back ndl as if to purl, leave st on ndl, go into first st on front ndl as if to knit, sl st off ndl, rep from * until all sts have been worked. Fasten off. ❖

Pompom Hat & Thumbless Mittens

Designs by Yarn by Mills

If your child loves color, this set is sure to please.

Experience Level
Intermediate***

Gauge
20 sts and 26 rows = 4 inches/10cm in St st

To save time, take time to check gauge.

Hat

Finished Size
Child's: one size fits most

Materials
- Yarn by Mills washable merino worsted weight yarn (125 yds/2 oz per skein): 4 oz variegated
- Size 7 (4.5mm) needles or size needed to obtain gauge
- Tapestry needle
- 3 x 7-inch piece of cardboard

CO 72 sts and work in k1, p1 ribbing until piece meas 1½ inches from beg.

Keeping first and last 4 sts in garter st, work rem sts in St st until piece meas 4½ inches.

Shape back
Continuing in St st, BO 4 sts at beg of every row until all sts are BO.

Fold hat in half with ribbing at front and sew BO edges tog.

Ties
Cut 9 (36-inch) strands, fold in half. Divide strands into 3 groups of 6 and braid. Secure ends and sew beg to front corner of hat. Rep for second tie.

Pompom
Wrap 100 turns of yarn around cardboard. Tie securely at one end, cut other end.

Approximately ¾ inch below top, wrap with another strand of yarn and fasten off. Trim ends. Sew pompom to top of hat.

Mittens

Finished Size
Approximately 3¼ inches wide at palm, 6½ inches long

Materials
- Yarn by Mills washable merino worsted weight yarn (125 yds/2 oz per skein): 1 oz variegated
- Size 7 (4.5mm) double-pointed needles or size needed to obtain gauge
- Tapestry needle

CO 32 sts and divide on dpns. Join without twisting and work in k1, p1 ribbing until piece meas 2 inches.

Change to St st and work until piece meas 5 inches from beg.

Shape top
Rnd 1: *K6, k2tog, rep from * around.

Rnd 2: *K5, k2tog, rep from * around.

Rnd 3: *K4, k2tog, rep from * around.

Rnd 4: *K3, k2tog, rep from * around.

Rnd 5: *K2, k2tog, rep from * around.

Rnd 6: *K1, k2tog, rep from * around. (8 sts rem)

Cut yarn. With tapestry needle, thread end through rem sts and fasten off.

Rep for second mitten.

Braid
Cut 18 (36-inch) strands. Divide strands into 3 groups of 6 and braid. Secure ends and sew a mitten on each end. ❖

Pigtail Cap

Design by Yarn by Mills

Here's a cute cap for an on-the-go kid. The braided pigtail on the top adds a touch of whimsy!

Experience Level
Intermediate***

Size
Child's: one size fits most

Finished Measurements
Approximately 16 inches x 8 inches high

Materials
- Yarn by Mills washable merino worsted weight yarn (125 yds/2 oz per skein): 2 oz pink (MC), 1 oz each yellow (A), aqua (B), ½ oz light blue (C)
- Size 5 (3.75mm) 16-inch circular needle
- Size 7 (4.5mm) double-pointed and 16-inch circular needles or size needed to obtain gauge
- Stitch marker
- Tapestry needle

Gauge
10 sts and 15 rnds = 2 inches/5cm in St st and color patt with larger ndls

To save time, take time to check gauge.

Pattern Note
Cap is worked in rnds of St st throughout.

When shaping top, change to dpn as needed.

With larger 16-inch ndl and MC, CO 80 sts. PM at beg of rnd and work 12 rnds.

Change to smaller ndl and work 2 rnds C, 8 rnds B, 2 rnds C.

Change to larger ndls

Rnds 1–4: With MC, knit.

Rnds 5–12: With MC and A, work Rnds 1–8 from Chart A.

Rnds 13–16: With MC, knit.

Rnds 17–20: With MC and B, work Rnds 1–4 from Chart B.

Rnds 21–23: With MC, knit.

Rnds 24–26: With MC and A, work Rnds 1–3 from Chart A.

Shape top
Rnds 1 and 2: With MC, work [k3, k2tog] around. (52 sts rem after Rnd 2)

Rnds 3–5: With MC and A, work Rnds 1–3 from Chart C.

Rnd 6: With B, work [k3, k2tog] around. (42 sts rem)

Rnd 7: With MC, knit.

Rnd 8: With MC, [k2tog] around. (21 sts)

Rnds 9 and 10: With B, knit.

Rnd 11: With MC, knit.

From this point, with MC, [k2tog] around until 6 sts rem. Cut yarn, pull end through rem sts and fasten off securely.

Pigtail
Cut 9 (14-inch) strands of yarn. Thread strands through top of hat, adjusting so ends are even. Divide into 3 groups of 6 strands and braid. Secure and trim ends. ❖

CHART A

Rep

CHART B

Rep

CHART C

Rep

COLOR KEY
- ☐ Pink (MC)
- ⊙ Yellow (A)
- ⦿ Aqua (B)

A Primary Work of Art

Design by Yarn by Mills

Worked from the top down, this cardigan comes to life with its clever two-colored seed stitch trim.

Experience Level
Intermediate***

Size
Child's 2(4)(6)(8) Instructions are given for smallest size, with larger sizes in parentheses. When only 1 number is given, it applies to all sizes.

Finished Measurements
Chest: 22(24)(26)(28½) inches
Length: 12(13½)(17½)(20) inches

Materials
- Yarn by Mills washable merino worsted weight yarn (500 yds/8 oz per skein): 8(8)(16)(16) oz solid blue (MC), 130 yds red (A), 25 yds yellow (B)
- Size 10½ (6.5mm) circular needle or size needed to obtain gauge
- Stitch markers
- Stitch holders
- 4(4)(5)(6) buttons

Gauge
14 sts and 21 rows = 4 inches/10cm in St st with 2 strands of yarn

To save time, take time to check gauge.

Pattern Notes
Sweater is worked with 2 strands of yarn held tog throughout.

Starting at neck, it is worked back and forth in rows and raglan shaping on a circular ndl, then divided for sleeves and body at underarm. Bands and cuffs are picked up in CC and worked in seed st.

Yoke
Beg at neck edge, with 2 strands of MC, CO 32(34)(36)(42) sts

Row 1 (WS): P2 (right front), pM, p6(6)(6)(8) (sleeve), pM, p16(18)(20)(22) (back), pM, p6(6)(6)(8) (sleeve), pM, p2 (left front). Do not join.

Row 2: Knit, inc 1 st before and after each marker. (8 sts inc; 40, 42, 44, 50 sts on ndl)

Row 3: Purl, inc 1 st at beg and end of row. (2 sts inc)

Row 4: Rep Row 2. (50, 52, 54, 60 sts)

Row 5: Purl.

Rep Rows 2–5 until there are 11(11)(13)(13) sts in each front section. At beg of next 2 rows, CO 3(4)(4)(5) sts for front neck.

Continue to work in rows of St st, inc 1 st before and after each marker eor until there are 38(42)(46)(50) sts in back. Yoke should meas approximately 5½(6)(6½)(6½) inches from beg.

Sleeve
Work to sleeve sts. Leaving rem sts for later, work even on sleeve sts for 1 inch.

Shape sleeve by dec 1 st at each side every inch until 26(28)(28)(30) sts rem. Work even until sleeve meas 6(7)(8)(9) inches or desired length from underarm.

Change to B and work 1 row. Change to A and work in seed st for 1½ inches. BO all sts in patt.

Attach yarn at underarm, work across back and complete 2nd sleeve as above.

Body
Attach yarn at underarm and work across rem front, then work all body sts in St st until body meas 9(11)(16)(18) inches from beg.

Change to B and work 1 row. Change to A and work in seed st for 1½ inches. BO all sts in patt.

Front Band
Note: *Work a swatch to determine gauge in seed st. CO 20 sts and work in seed st for several rows, then BO all sts. Lay swatch along neck edge and mark beg and end of swatch*

with pins. Place another pin in center of this distance. Mark this spacing around front and neck edges, then pick up and k 10 sts in each space.

With B, pick up and k sts as above along front and neck edges. Change to A and work in seed st until band meas approximately ¾ inch. Work 4(4)(5)(6) buttonholes evenly spaced bet bottom and beg of neck shaping in right or left front, then work in est patt until band meas 1½ inches. BO all sts in patt.

Finishing

Sew sleeve seams. Sew buttons opposite buttonholes. Block lightly. ❖

Blocks & Dots

Design by E. J. Slayton

Knit these socks in your kids' favorite colors or in their school colors. Either way, they'll be a hit with the younger set.

Experience Level
Intermediate***

Size
Child's small(medium)(large)(extra-large) Instructions are given for smallest size, with larger sizes in parentheses. When only 1 number is given, it applies to all sizes.

Finished Measurements
Top: 4¾(5½)(6)(6½) inches

Foot length: 6½(7)(7½)(8½) inches

Materials
- Brown Sheep Company Nature Spun 100 percent wool sport weight yarn (184 yds/50g per skein): 1(1)(2)(2) skeins Peruvian pink #N85 (MC), 1 skein each sapphire #N65 (A), natural #730 (B)
- Size 2 (2.75mm) double-pointed needles or size needed to obtain gauge
- Heel and toe reinforcement or Wooly Nylon (optional)
- Stitch markers
- Safety pin
- Tapestry needle

Gauge
14 sts and 17 rnds = 2 inches/5cm in St st

To save time, take time to check gauge.

Sock
With MC, CO 40(44)(48)(52) sts and join, being careful not to twist. Work in k2, p2 rib until cuff meas 1½(1½)(2)(2) inches. K 2 rnds.

Beg patt
Work color patt from Chart A until top meas 4¾(5½)(6) (6½) inches or desired length from beg.

Heel
Using MC only, work across next 11(12)(13)(14) sts. Divide next 19(21)(23)(25) sts bet 2 ndls for instep, sl rem 10(11)(12)(13) sts to beg of first ndl. P21(23)(25)(27) heel sts.

Row 1: Sl 1, *k1, sl 1, rep from * across.

Row 2: Purl.

Rows 3–19(21)(23)(25): Rep Rows 1 and 2, ending with Row 1. (10, 11, 12, 13 loops on each side of heel flap)

Shape heel
Row 1: P13(15)(16)(17), p2tog, turn.

Row 2: Sl 1, k5(7)(7)(7), ssk, turn.

Row 3: Sl 1, p5(7)(7)(7), p2tog, turn.

Rep Rows 2 and 3 until center 7(9)(9)(9) sts rem.

Instep
With ndl containing heel sts, pick up and k 10(11)(12)(13) sts along edge of heel flap (Ndl 1); k19(21)(23)(25) for instep (Ndl 2); pick up and k 10(11)12)(13) sts along edge of heel flap, with same ndl, k 3(4)(4)(4) heel sts from Ndl 1 (Ndl 3). (46, 52,

56, 60 sts)

Rnd 1: Knit.

Rnd 2: K to 3 sts from end of Ndl 1, k2tog, k1; k across Ndl 2; on Ndl 3, k1, ssk, k to end.

[Work Rnds 1 and 2] 4(5)(5)(5) times. (19, 21, 23, 25 sts rem on Ndls 1 and 3)

Work even until foot meas 5(5½)(6)(7) inches or approximately 1½ inches less than desired length.

Toe

Rnd 1: K to 3 sts from end of Ndl 1, k2tog, k1; on Ndl 2, k1, ssk, k to last 3 sts, k2tog, k1; on Ndl 3, k1, ssk, k to end.

Rnd 2: Knit.

Rep Rnds 1 and 2 until 22 sts rem. With Ndl 3, k across sts from Ndl 1.

Weave toe

Cut yarn, leaving an 18-inch end. Thread yarn in tapestry ndl, hold ndls holding sts parallel, *insert ndl in first st on front ndl as if to purl, leave st on ndl, go into first st on back ndl as if to knit, sl st off ndl, go into next st on back ndl as if to purl, leave st on ndl, go into first st on front ndl as if to knit, sl st off ndl, rep from * until all sts have been worked. Fasten off. ❖

CHART A

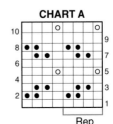

COLOR KEY

- □ MC
- ▣ A
- ◉ B

Rep

His & Her Baby Socks

Design by E. J. Slayton

Knit these adorable his and her socks for your little ones to wear. You'll want to make them in a variety of colors.

Experience Level
Intermediate***

Size
To fit 3–6 mos(12–18 mos)(2T) Instructions are given for smallest size, with larger sizes in parentheses. When only 1 number is given, it applies to all sizes.

Finished Measurements
Top: 3(3½)(4) inches

Foot length: 4½(5½)(6) inches

Materials
• Brown Sheep Company Cotton Fine 80 percent pima cotton/20 percent merino wool fingering weight yarn (222 yds/50g per skein): 1 skein pink diamond #222
• Size 0 (2mm) double-pointed needles or size needed to obtain gauge
• Stitch markers
• Safety pin
• Tapestry needle

Gauge
17 sts = 2 inches/5 cm in St st

To save time, take time to check gauge.

Pattern Notes
To make sock, knit specified number of reps of edging for chosen size, join beg to end, then pick up and k 1 st in each sl st of edging and work rest of sock.

When working edging, sl sts purlwise with yarn in front, then take yarn to back bet tips of ndls. For heel flap, sl sts purlwise with yarn in back.

For plain sock, skip edging, CO 40(44)(48) sts and follow instructions from beg of ribbing, adjusting length of top if desired.

Lace Edging
CO 6 sts.

Row 1: Sl 1, k2tog, yo, k1, yo, k2. (7 sts)

Rows 2, 4 and 6: Knit.

Row 3: Sl 1, k2tog, yo, [k1, yo] twice, k2. (9 sts)

Row 5: Sl 1, k2tog, yo, [k1, yo] 4 times, k2. (13 sts)

Row 7: Sl 1, k2tog, yo, k10.

Row 8: BO7, k to end. (6 sts)

Rep Rows 1–8 for edging.

Sock
Work 10(11)(12) reps of edging, do not cut yarn. Join beg and end of edging, with RS facing, pick up and k 1 st in each sl st loop around edging. (40, 44, 48 sts)

Join and k 2 rnds. Sl first st of next rnd, bring yarn to front, return st to left ndl, take yarn to back and flip work around ndls. You will now be working in opposite direction.

Beg k2, p2 rib, working st and wrap tog at end of first rnd. Continue to work in rib until top meas 3(3½)(4) inches or desired length from beg, ending 1(2)(3) sts before end of rnd.

Heel
Beg p1(p2)(k1, p2), k2, work next 20(22)(24) sts onto 1 ndl for heel, divide rem 20(22)(24) sts bet 2 ndls for instep.

Work in St st on heel sts only for 20(22)(24) rows, sl first and last st every RS row and ending with a RS row.

Shape heel
Place safety pin bet st #10 (11)(12) and next st. Shaping will take place evenly spaced on each side of marker.

Row 1: Sl 1, p12(13)(14), p2tog, p1, turn.

Row 2: Sl 1, k5, k2tog, k1, turn.

Row 3: Sl 1, p6, p2tog, p1, turn.

Row 4: Sl 1, k7, k2tog, k1, turn.

Continue to work back and forth in this manner, having 1 more st before dec until all sts

have been worked. (12, 14, 14 heel sts rem)

Instep

Using ndl containing rem heel sts, pick up and k 10(11)(12) sts along edge of heel flap (Ndl 1); k3(4)(5), pM, work 14 sts in est rib, pM, k3(4)(5) (Ndl 2); pick up and k 10(11)(12) sts along edge of heel flap, work 6(7)(7) sts from Ndl 1 (Ndl 3). (52, 58, 62 sts)

Rnd 1: K to marker, work in est rib to next marker, k to end.

Rnd 2: K to 3 sts from end of Ndl 1, k2tog, k1; work in est patt across Ndl 2; on Ndl 3, k1, ssk, k to end.

Rep Rnds 1 and 2 until a total of 20(22)(24) sts rem on Ndls 1 and 3, then work even as est until foot meas 3½ (4½)(5) inches or approximately 1 inch less than desired length.

Toe

Rnd 1: K to 3 sts from end of Ndl 1, k2tog, k1; on Ndl 2, k1, ssk, k to last 3 sts, k2tog, k1; on Ndl 3, k1, ssk, k to end.

Rnd 2: Knit.

Rep Rnds 1 and 2 until 20 sts rem, ending with Rnd 1. With Ndl 3, k across sts from Ndl 1. (10 sts on each ndl)

Weave toe

Cut yarn, leaving a 12-inch end. Thread yarn in tapestry ndl, hold ndls holding sts parallel, *insert ndl in first st on front ndl as if to purl, leave st on ndl, go into first st on back ndl as if to knit, sl st off ndl, go into next st on back ndl as if to purl, leave st on ndl, go into first st on front ndl as if to knit, sl st off ndl, rep from * until all sts have been worked. Fasten off. ❖

Back-to-School Pouch

Design by Barbara Venishnick

Knit a pouch that is perfect for school or traveling.
The small pockets are just right for tiny treasures.

Experience Level
Intermediate***

Finished Size
Approximately 12 inches tall x 11 inches wide x 2 inches deep

Materials
- Dale of Norway Free Style 100 percent machine washable wool worsted weight yarn (86 yds/50g per skein): 3 skeins natural #0020 (A), 3 skeins lime #9133 (B), 4 skeins turquoise #6135 (C), 2 skeins hot pink #4417 (D)
- Size 5 (3.75mm) straight, 29-inch circular and 2 double-pointed needles or size needed to obtain gauge
- 2 pair (3⁄4-inch) hook-and-loop dot fasteners
- Tapestry needle

Gauge
20 stitches and 40 rows = 4 inches/10cm in twisted garter st

To save time, take time to check gauge.

Pattern Stitch
Twisted Garter Stitch
Knit every stitch through back loop.

Back
With A and straight ndls, CO 58 sts.

Working in patt, k 2 rows B, then 2 rows A alternately until piece meas 12 inches, ending with 2 rows of A. Sl all sts to circular ndl and leave for later.

Flap
With A and straight ndls, CO 22 sts. Work in patt and color sequence as for back. *At the same time,* inc 1 st on each side [every RS row] 18 times. Work even on 58 sts for 2 inches, ending with 2 rows of color A. Do not cut yarn.

Join flap to back
Place flap over back with WS tog. With B, k2tog across (1 st from flap tog with 1 st from back).

Turn and k 1 row with B, 2 rows with A, 1 row with B.

Divide for straps
With WS facing and B, k20, join a second ball of yarn, BO 18, k20, turn.

Continue in est color sequence, working both straps at the same time with separate balls of yarn.

Dec 1 st at neck (center)

edge of each strap [every RS row] 7 times, then dec 1 st at shoulder edge of each strap [every RS row] twice.

Work even on 11 sts for each strap for 12 inches. BO all sts leaving a 12-inch tail for sewing.

Main Pouch
With C and straight ndls, CO 58 sts.

Work in twisted garter st for 20 rows.

At beg of next 2 rows, CO 11 sts. (80 sts)

Form fold lines
Row 1 (RS): K11, sl 1, k56, sl 1, k11.

Row 2: K11, p1, k56, p1, k11.

Rep Rows 1 and 2 until piece meas 11¾ inches from beg of fold lines.

Eyelet row (RS): K1, k2tog, *yo, k1, k2tog, rep from * across, end last rep yo, k2.

Next row (WS): [K2, p1] across, end k2

Knit 1 row on RS. BO all sts knitwise.

Sew CO sts to first 20 rows of pouch on each side to form a box.

Small Pockets
Make 1 A and 1 B

CO 15 sts and work in patt for 6 rows.

At beg of next 2 rows, CO 3 sts. (21 sts)

Row 1 (RS): K3, sl 1, k13, sl 1, k3.

Row 2: K3, p1, k13, p1, k3.

Rep Rows 1 and 2 until piece meas 2¾ inches above CO row, ending with a RS row. BO all sts knitwise.

Sew CO sts to first 6 rows of pocket.

Small Flaps
Make 2

With D, CO 15 sts. Work in patt for 10 rows.

Dec 1 st each side [every RS row] 4 times. With WS facing, BO rem 7 sts knitwise.

Finishing
Small pockets

Place lower left corner of 1 pocket 9 sts in from fold edge and 9 garter ridges up from bottom fold. Pin in place, then sew sides and bottom of pocket to main pouch.

Place lower right corner of second pocket 9 sts in from fold edge and 9 garter ridges up from bottom fold. Pin in place then sew sides and bottom of pocket to main pouch.

Place a small flap across top opening of each small pocket. Pin with wide edge 1 garter ridge above top opening of pocket. Sew in place.

Sew a pair of hook and loop dots to each pocket and flap for closure.

Join main pouch to back

Place pouch over back with WS tog, pin in place. Hold with pouch on top. Beg at upper corner, with 29-inch circular ndl and D and working through both layers throughout, pick up and k 1 st in each valley bet garter ridges along side of pouch; pick up and k 1 st in each CO st across bottom

Fig. 1

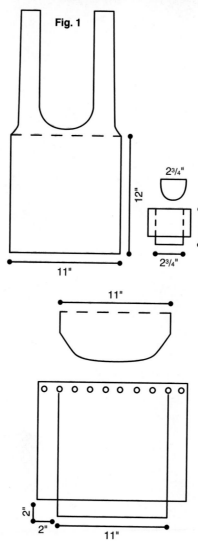

12"

11"

2¾"

3"

2¾"

11"

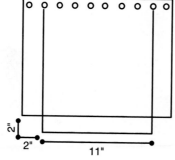

2"

2"

11"

of pouch; work up other side as for first side.

Turn and work 6 rows of reverse St st, beg with a knit row. BO all sts knitwise. Cut

yarn, leaving a long tail. Allow St st trim to curl over seam. Using long tail, sew BO edge to purl bumps of pick-up row on back of bag.

Trim for straps

With D and 29-inch circular ndl, hold bag with RS facing, beg at end of 1 strap on inside edge, pick up and k 1 st in each valley bet garter ridges along edge of strap; pick up and k 1 st in each BO st across back neck opening; work down edge of other strap as for other side.

Turn and work 4 rows of reverse St st, beg with a knit row. Complete as for main section.

With D and 29-inch circular ndl, hold bag with RS facing, beg at end of 1 strap on outside edge, pick up and k 1 st in each valley bet garter ridges along edge of strap and side of large flap; pick up and k 1 st in each CO st of large flap; work along other edge of flap and other strap as for first side.

Work trim as for inside edge of straps.

I-Cord Ties
Make 1 A, 1 B

With dpn, CO 4 sts. Do not turn.*Sl sts to other end of ndl, pull yarn across back, k4, rep from * until cord meas 15 inches.

Cut yarn and thread through a tapestry ndl, draw through rem sts, fasten off and thread end inside I-Cord.

Sew each I-Cord to inside of main pouch next to row of yo eyelets. Thread cord through eyelets, each color halfway around. Tie a knot at end of each cord. Tie both cords tog to close pouch. ❖

Edelweiss Winter Dress

Design by Dawn Brocco

Your little princess will look delightful in this beautiful dress.
A simple crochet edge adds the finishing touch.

Experience Level
Intermediate***

Size
Child's size 1(2)(3)(4) Instructions are given for smallest size, with larger sizes in parentheses. When only 1 number is given, it applies to all sizes.

Finished Measurements
Chest: 22(25)(26)(27) inches
Length: 16(17½)(19½)(21) inches
Sleeve: 8½(9½)(10½)(11½) inches
Armhole Depth: 5(5)(6)(6) inches

Materials
- JCA/Reynolds Inc. Dover 100 percent washable wool heavy worsted weight yarn (82 yds/1¾ oz per skein): 5(5)(6)(7) skeins sage #27 (A), 2(2)(3)(3) skeins natural #04 (B)
- Size 8 (5mm) double-pointed and 24-inch circular needles or size needed to obtain gauge
- Stitch holders
- Size G/6 (4mm) crochet hook

Gauge
18 sts and 23 rnds = 4 inches/ 10 cm in St st.

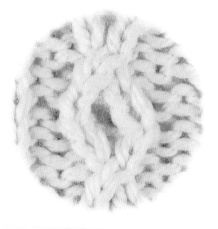

To save time, take time to check gauge.

Special Abbreviations
Skp: Sl 2 sts tog knitwise, k1, pass 2 slipped sts over k1.

T2B: K into front of 2nd st on LH ndl, then p1 in first st, sl both sts off ndl tog.

T2F: P into back of 2nd st on LH ndl, then k1 in first st, sl both sts off ndl tog.

C2B: K into front of 2nd st on LH ndl, then k1 in first st, sl both sts off ndl tog.

Pattern Stitch
(Multiple of 9 sts)
Row 1 (RS): P1, k1, p1, T2B, T2F, p1, k1.
Row 2 (WS): P1, k1, p1, k2, [p1, k1] twice.
Row 3: P1, k1, p1, T2F, T2B, p1, k1.
Row 4: P1, k2, p2, k2, p1, k1.
Row 5: P1, k1, p2, C2B, p2, k1.

Row 6: Rep Row 4.
Rep Rows 1–6 for patt.

Body
With circular ndl and A, CO 150(168)(174)(186) sts. Join without twisting and k 50 (60)(65)(75) rnds. (8¾, 10½, 11½, 13 inches)

Next rnd: *K3, skp, rep from * around. (100, 112, 116, 124 sts rem)

With B, k 1 rnd, p 1 rnd.

Color patt
Rnd 1: With B, knit.

Rnd 2: With B, purl.

Rnds 3 and 4: *K2 B, k2 A, rep from * around.

Rnds 5 and 6: *K2 A, k2 B, rep from * around.

Rnd 7: With A, knit.

Rnd 8: With A, purl.

Back
With A, turn and p50(p2tog, p54)(p2tog, p56)(p62). (50, 55, 57, 62 sts)

Place rem 50(56)(58)(62) sts on holder for front.

Set up patt
Size 1: P1, k1, [work patt rep] 5 times, end p1, k1, p1.

Size 2: [Work patt rep] 6 times, end p1.

Size 3: K1, [work patt rep] 6 times, end p1, k1.

Size 4: K1, p1, T2B, T2F, p1, k1, [work patt rep] 6 times.

Work 30(30)(36)(36) rows in est patt, dec 1(0)(0)(1) st in center of last row.

Mark center 23 sts for back neck, place all sts on holder.

Front

With WS facing, p50(p2tog, p54)(p2tog, p56)(p62). (50, 55, 57, 62 sts)

Set up patt as for back and work 18(18)(24)(24) rows, ending with a WS row, and dec 1(0)(0)(1) st in center of last row.

Shape left neck

Work first 17(20)(21)(23) sts in est patt, place next 15 sts on holder, leave right neck sts for later. Maintaining est patt throughout, turn and work 1 row.

Next row: Work to last 3 sts, k2tog, k1.

Continuing in patt, dec 1 st at neck edge every 3rd row until 14(17)(18)(20) shoulder sts rem, then work even until front meas same as back to shoulder.

Shape right neck

With RS facing, join yarns at neck edge and work 2 rows in patt.

At beg of next row, k1, ssk, complete row. Complete as for left neck, reversing shaping.

BO front and back shoulder sts tog as follows:

Hold ndls containing shoulder sts parallel, right sides tog; with 3rd ndl, k first st on front and back ndls tog, *k next st on both ndls tog, BO 1, rep from * until all sts are worked, fasten off. Rep for 2nd shoulder.

Sleeves

With A and dpns, beg at center underarm, pick up and k 1 st at center underarm and 46(46)(56)(56) sts evenly around armhole. P 1 rnd.

Work color patt Rnds 3–6 as for body, then work Rnds 7 and 8 with A.

With B, k, dec 1 st at each side of center underarm st every 5th rnd until 31(29)(37)(35) sts rem.

Next rnd: K, dec 6(4)(7)(5) sts evenly around. (25, 25, 30, 30 sts rem)

Sleeve Trim

Rnd 1: With crochet hook and A, work 1 sc into each st around, sl st to first sc, ch 1, turn.

Rnd 2: Sc around, sl st to beg, ch 1, turn.

Rnd 3: With B, work 3 sc, *ch 5, sl st to first ch, work 5 sc, rep from * around, end with 2 sc, sl st to first sc. Fasten off.

Lower Edge Trim

Work as for sleeve trim.

Neck Trim

With RS facing, crochet hook and B, sc across 23 neck back sts, work 11 sc along left neck edge, sc across 15 front neck sts, and 11 sc along right neck edge. (60 sts)

Complete as for sleeve trim, reversing colors. ❖

A-B-C, 1-2-3 Overalls Set

Design by Diane Zangl

This colorful three-piece wardrobe for toddlers is worked in small, portable pieces and basic stitches.

Experience Level
Intermediate***

Size
Toddler size 1(2)(3)
Instructions are given for smallest size, with larger sizes in parentheses. When only one number is given it applies to all sizes. Allowance is made for diapers.

Materials
- Plymouth Wildflower DK weight yarn 51 percent cotton/49 percent acrylic (137 yds/50g per ball): 4(4)(5) balls red #46, 3(3)(4) balls each blue #57 and yellow #48, 2 balls green #49
- Size 4 (3.5mm) needles
- Size 5 (3.75mm) needles
- Size F/5 (3.75mm) crochet hook
- Stitch holders
- Stitch markers
- 6 (⅝-inch) buttons, JHB International #42450
- Elastic thread (optional)
- Small amount of polyester fiberfill

Gauge
22 sts and 28 rows = 4 inches/10 cm in St st with larger ndls

25 sts and 32 rows = 4 inches/10 cm in twisted St st with smaller ndls

To save time, take time to check gauge.

Pattern Stitches
Twisted Rib (worked in rows)
Row 1(RS): K1b, *p1, k1b, rep from * across row.

Row 2: P1b, *k1, p1b, rep from * across row.

Rep Rows 1 and 2 for patt.

Twisted Rib (worked in rnds)

*K1b, pl. Rep from * on every rnd.

Twisted Stockinette

Row 1(RS): Knit in back of all sts.

Row 2: Purl in back of all sts.

Rep Rows 1 and 2 for patt.

Color Stripe Sequence
Work 2 rows each of yellow, green, blue, red.

Raglan dec row (RS): K1, ssk, k to last 3 sts, k2tog, k1.

Pullover
Finished Measurements
Chest: 22(24)(26) inches

Armhole depth: 5(5½)(6) inches

Length to underarm: 8(9)(10) inches

Sleeve length: 7(9)(10) inches

Pattern Note
Do not cut yarns when working color stripe patt, carry along edge of work. End sleeves and back with same color at underarm.

Back
With smaller ndls and red, CO 61(67)(71) sts. Work even in twisted rib for 1½ inches. Change to larger ndls. Work even in St st and color stripe patt until back meas 8(9)(10) inches, end WS.

Shape raglan sleeve
BO 8(8)(9) sts at beg of next 2 rows. (45, 51, 53 sts)

Work raglan dec row every 4th row 4(4)(5) times, then eor 9(11)(11) times. Sl rem 19(21)(21) sts to holder.

Front
Work as for back until 7(9)(10) raglan decs have been completed, end WS.

Shape neck
K11(12)(12) sts, sl next 9(11)(11) sts to one holder and rem 11(12)(12) sts to second holder. Working on left side of neck only, dec 1 st at neck edge every row 4 times, *at the same time*, continue raglan decs until armhole meas same as for back. Fasten off rem st. Sl sts from 2nd holder to larger ndl. With RS facing, join yarn at neck edge. Work right side of neck as for left, reversing shaping.

Fig. 1

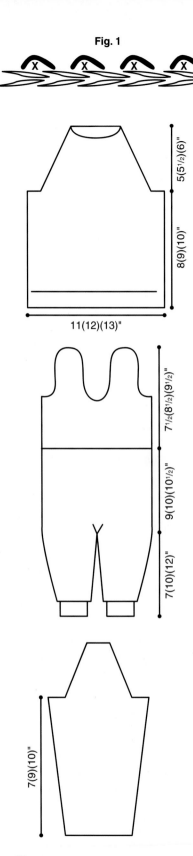

Pick up in P Bump (X)

11(12)(13)"

5(5½)(6)"

8(9)(10)"

7½(8½)(9½)"

9(10)(10½)"

7(10)(12)"

7(9)(10)"

Fig. 2

1			
Stripe			

2	A	B	C
Red	Blue	Green	Yellow

			3
			Stripe

Work in St st and color stripe patt, inc 1 st each side [alternating every 2 rows, then every 4 rows] 5 times, then every 2 rows 0(1)(1) time. (48, 54, 58 sts)

Work even until sleeve meas approximately 7(9)(10) inches, ending with WS and same color stripe as on body.

Shape raglan

BO 8(8)(9) sts at beg of next 2 rows. Dec 1 st each end every 4th row 4(4)(5) times, then eor 9(11)(11) times. Sl rem 6(8)(8) sts to holder.

Sew right sleeve to front and back. Sew left sleeve to back only. Leaving top 3 inches of seam unsewn, sew rem seam.

Button band

With yellow, work 1 row sc across back section of open sleeve seam, making sure to keep work flat.

Buttonhole band

With smaller ndls and yellow, join yarn at bottom of neck opening. Pick up and k 1 st in each row. Work 2 rows twisted rib. Mark band for 3 buttons, top one will be on neck band and remainder on k sts evenly spaced.

Buttonhole Row(WS):

[Work to marker, yo, k2tog] twice, work to end of row. Work 2 rows even. BO in patt. Do not cut yarn, leave last st on RH ndl.

Neck band

Pick up and k 4 sts along end of buttonhole band, 12 sts along left side of neck, k9(11)(11) sts of front neck, pick up and k 12 sts along right side of neck, k6(8)(8) sts of right sleeve, 19(21)(21) sts of back neck, 6(8)(8) sts of left sleeve. (69, 77, 77 sts)

Making final buttonhole on first row, work in twisted rib patt for 5 rows. BO in patt.

Finishing

Sew sleeve and side seams. Sew on buttons.

Overalls
Finished Measurements
Back neck to waist: 7½(8½)(9½) inches

Waist to crotch: 9(10)(10½) inches

Inseam: 7(10)(12) inches

Pattern Note

For easier working of edging around top of overalls, *pick up and k a small number of sts at a time with one strand of yarn. Using another strand of yarn for BO, rep from * around. Pick up at a ratio of 3 sts for every 4 rows and 1 st in every BO st.

Sleeves

With smaller ndls and red, CO 25(29)(31) sts. Work even in twisted rib for 1½ inches, changing to larger ndls and inc 3(3)(5) sts on last row. (28, 32, 36 sts)

Left Leg

With smaller ndls and green, CO 43(49)(51) sts. Work even in twisted rib for 2 inches, inc 14(17)(18) sts evenly on last row. (57, 66, 69 sts)

Change to larger ndls and blue. Work in St st, inc 1 st each side [every 4th row] 9(11)(11) times. Work even on 75(88)(91) sts until leg meas 7(10)(12) inches, ending with a WS row.

Shape crotch

BO 3(6)(6) sts at beg of next 2 rows. Dec 1 st each side eor 3(5)(5) times. (63, 66, 69 sts)

Work even until leg meas 8(9)(9½) inches above BO crotch sts, dec 5(5)(6) sts on last WS row. Sl sts to holder.

Right Leg

Work as for left leg, substituting yellow for cuff and red for rem.

Body

Work in rnds from this point. Sl leg sts to smaller ndls. With RS facing, join green and knit 1 rnd, pM between first and last st. This will be center back seam. Work even in twisted rib for 1 inch. Change to larger ndls and yellow. Inc 10(10)(12) sts on first rnd, work even in St st for 1½(2)(2½) inches. (126, 132, 138 sts)

Divide for front and back

PM after sts 32(33)(35) and 94(99)(103). (62, 66, 68 front sts; 64, 66, 70 back sts)

Next rnd: K to 4(5)(5) sts before marker, BO 8(10)(10) sts for left underarm, k54(56)(58) sts and place on holder, BO 8(10)(10) sts for right underarm, knit to end of rnd.

Back

Work in rows from this point. Dec 1 st each side eor 5 times. (44, 46, 48 sts)

Work even until back meas 4½(5½)(6½) inches above waist, ending with a WS row.

Shape neck and straps

K13, join 2nd ball of yarn and BO next 18(20)(22) sts, k13. Working on both straps simultaneously with separate balls of yarn, dec 1 st each side of neck [every row] 3 times. (10 sts in each strap)

Work even until straps meas 3 inches. Dec 1 st each side of strap [every row] twice. BO rem 6 sts.

Front

Sl sts from holder to larger ndl. With RS facing, join yellow at left underarm. Work as for back until front meas 3½(4½)(5½) inches above waist, ending with a WS row.

Shape neck and straps

K13, join 2nd ball of yarn and BO next 16(20)(20) sts, k13. Working on both straps simultaneously with separate balls of yarn, dec 1 st each side of neck every row 3 times. (10 sts in each strap)

Work even until straps meas 3½ inches, ending with a WS row.

Buttonhole row (RS): K4, yo, k2tog, k4.

Work even until straps meas same as back straps above underarm. Dec 1 st each side [every row] twice. BO rem sts.

Pocket

With smaller ndls and red, CO 25 sts. Work even in St st for 2½ inches, ending with a WS row.

Buttonhole row: K12, yo, k2tog, k to end of row.

Purl 1 row. BO all sts. Sew pocket to front of overalls.

Edging

With smaller ndls and green, beg at underarm, pick up and k around top edge of overalls (see note). BO all sts. With blue, pick up and k 1 st in purl bump of each st of BO row (see Fig. 1). BO all sts.

Finishing

Sew center front and back seams. Sew leg seams. Sew on buttons. If desired, run elastic thread through waistband ribbing

Block

Finished Size

Approximately 4 inches square

Pattern Note

Block is worked entirely in twisted St st unless noted otherwise. To avoid holes when working color sections, always pick up new color from under old. Gauge is not critical, but sts should be worked firmly to avoid polyfill showing through.

With smaller ndls and yellow, CO 25 sts. Work in color stripe sequence and twisted St st patt until block meas 4 inches, ending with a WS row. Change to yellow. Knit 1 row untwisted, do not turn. CO at end of row 25 sts each green, blue and red. (100 sts)

Knit 1 row untwisted. Next row: Working in est colors [P1, sl 1, k23b] 4 times.

Row 2: [P24b, p1, k1] 4 times.

Rep these 2 rows until solid-color sections meas 4 inches, ending with a RS row. Knit 1 row untwisted.

Next row: BO 75 sts, with yellow knit to end of row. (25 sts)

Work in color stripe sequence until striped section meas 4 inches, ending with a WS row. BO all sts.

Continued on page 117

Felted Grape Purse

Design by Kathleen Brklacich Sasser

Decorate with a special button and delight the little girl in your life!

Experience Level
Beginner*

Finished Size
Approximately 5½ x 4½ inches Size may vary in felting.

Materials
- Bryspun Kid-n-Ewe 50 percent kid mohair/50 percent wool worsted weight yarn (120 yds/50g per skein): 1 skein #420 (A), 1 skein #230 (B)
- Size 10 (6mm) needles
- Size 10½ (6.5mm) needles or size needed to obtain gauge
- Tapestry needle
- 1 (1½-inch) button

Gauge
Approximately 13 sts and 24 rows = 4 inches/10cm in garter st with larger ndls

To save time, take time to check gauge.

Pattern Note
Purse is worked with 2 strands held tog throughout.

With larger ndls and 2 strands held tog, CO 20 sts.

Work in garter st until piece meas 10 inches from beg.

Mark each end of last row with scrap yarn.

Shape flap
Dec 1 st at each side [eor] 4 times. (12 sts rem)

Buttonhole row: K3, BO 6 sts, k2. (3 sts on each side)

Next row: K3, CO 6 sts, k3.

K 5 more rows, then BO knitwise.

Finishing
Fold piece, bringing CO edge up to marked row. Sew side seams, removing markers.

I-Cord Strap
With smaller ndls, CO 3 sts, do not turn. *Sl sts to other end of ndl, pull yarn across back, k3, rep from * until cord meas approximately 45 inches. Cut yarn and thread through sts, fasten off.

Sew strap to inside of purse at top of each side seam.

Felting
Machine-wash on hot wash/cold rinse cycle, allowing it to agitate several cycles. You may prefer to reset cycle rather than allowing machine to refill each time. Continue until garter st ridges are no longer distinct and piece is fuzzy. Shape and allow to dry thoroughly. Attach button. ❖

A-B-C, 1-2-3 Overall Set
Continued from page 115

Finishing
With CC of your choice, embroider letters and numbers to each section of block (see Fig. 2). Sew bottom striped section to solid color sections on 3 sides. Stuff with polyfill. Sew rem 3 sides of upper stripe section. ❖

Afghans on the Go

*Y*ou may think you don't have time to knit an afghan, but the designs in this chapter can be knit in strips or squares. Knit a strip when you're waiting for an appointment or a square during those extra moments at lunchtime. Soon you'll have a warm and cozy afghan and a pillow to match.

Chapter 4

Malibu Chains Afghan

Design by Barbara Venishnick

This very portable two-color project is easier to knit than it looks.

Experience Level
Intermediate***

Afghan

Finished Size
Approximately 43 x 57 inches (excluding tassels)

Materials
- Brown Sheep Co. Cotton Fleece 80 percent pima cotton/20 percent merino wool worsted weight yarn (215 yds/100g per skein): 9 skeins antique lace #CW 150 (A), 8 skeins Malibu blue #CW 570 (B)
- Size 6 (4mm) needles or size needed to obtain gauge
- Cable needle

Gauge
Each strip meas 2⅛ inches wide x 57 inches long in patt

To save time, take time to check gauge.

Pattern Notes
Each 2-color strip is worked separately, then sewed tog.

Sl all sts as if to purl with yarn in back on RS rows and in front on WS rows.

Special Abbreviations
Cable 3 front (c3f): Sl 2 sts to cn, hold in front, k1, k2 from cn.

Cable 3 back (c3b): Sl 1 st to cn, hold in back, k2, k1 from cn.

Cable 5 back (c5b): Sl 3 sts to cn, hold in back, k2, pass cn bet ndls to front of work, sl 3rd st (MC) on cn back to left ndl, transfer this st, unworked, to RH ndl, k2 from cn. (this keeps central MC st bet 2 crossed arms of cable)

Pattern Stitch
With A, CO 17 sts and knit 1 row.

Row 1 (RS): With B, k6, sl 2, k1, sl 2, k6.

Row 2: With B, p1, k5, sl 2, k1, sl 2, k5, p1.

Row 3: With A, [k1, sl 1] 3 times, c5b, [sl 1, k1] 3 times.

Row 4: With A, p1, [sl 1, k1] twice, [sl 1, p2] twice, [sl 1, k1] twice, sl 1, p1.

Rows 5 and 6: Rep Rows 1 and 2.

Row 7: With A, k2, sl 1, k1, sl 1, c3b, sl 1, c3f, [sl 1, k1] twice, k1.

Row 8: With A, p1, [k1, sl 1] twice, p2, k1, sl 1, k1, p2, [sl 1, k1] twice, p1.

Row 9: With B, k5, sl 2, k3, sl 2, k5.

Row 10: With B, p1, k4, sl 2, k3, sl 2, k4, p1.

Row 11: With A, [k1, sl 1] twice, c3b, sl 1, k1, sl 1, c3f, [sl 1, k1] twice.

Row 12: With A, p1, sl 1, k1, sl 1, p2, [k1, sl 1] twice, k1, p2, sl 1, k1, sl 1, p1.

Row 13: With B, k4, sl 2, k5, sl 2, k4.

Row 14: With B, p1, k3, sl 2, k5, sl 2, k3, p1.

Row 15: With A, k2, sl 1, k3, [sl 1, k1] twice, sl 1, k3, sl 1.

Row 16: With A, p1, k1, sl 1, k1, p2, [sl1, k1] twice, sl 1, p2, k1, sl 1, k1, p1.

Rows 17 and 18: Rep Rows 13 and 14.

Row 19: With A, [k1, sl 1] twice, c3f, sl 1, k1, sl 1, c3b, [sl 1, k1] twice.

Row 20: With A, p1, [sl 1, k1] twice, p2, sl 1, k1, sl1, p2, [k1, sl 1] twice, p1.

Rows 21 and 22: Rep Rows 9 and 10.

Row 23: With B, k1, [k1, sl 1] twice, c3f, sl1, c3b, [sl 1, k1] twice, k1.

Row 24: With B, p1, [k1, sl 1] twice, k1, p2, sl 1, p2, [k1, sl 1] twice, k1, p1.

Rep Rows 1–24 for patt.

Afghan
Make 18 strips

With A, CO 17 sts and knit 1 row. Work [Rows 1–24 of patt] 23 times. [Rep Rows 1–4] once more. BO all sts with A.

Sew strips tog.

Tassels

Make 36

With A, cut 23 (11-inch) strands. Tie them tog in center using another 11-inch strand of A. Fold in half at tied point and wrap color B several times around entire bundle 3⁄4 inch down from top. Tie securely and bury ends of color B inside tassel. With long ends of tie, sew tassel to end of a cable. Rep for both ends of each cable.

Make 8 strips

CO 17 sts with A. Knit 1 row.

Beg with Row 13, work

Bolster Pillow

Finished Size

21 inches long x 21 inches in circumference

Materials

• Brown Sheep Co Cotton Fleece 80 percent pima cotton/20 percent merino wool worsted weight yarn (215 yds/100g per skein): 2 skeins antique lace #CW

Rows 13–24, [Rows 1–24] 7 times, then [Rows 1–12] once more. BO all sts with A.

Sew strips tog.

150 (A), 2 skeins Malibu blue #CW 570 (B)

• 1 Size 3 (3.25mm) or smaller needle for making tuck
• Size 6 (4mm) needles or size needed to obtain gauge
• Cable needle
• Tapestry needle
• 12 oz bag of polyester fiberfill

Side Trim and End

With A and RS facing, pick up and k 98 sts along side of first

Continued on page 141

Candy Rainbow Baby Afghan

Design by Nazanin S. Fard

This simple afghan uses only knit and purl stitches. Its rainbow of color will attract the eye of your little one.

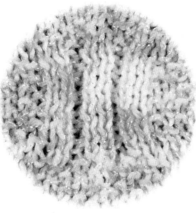

Experience Level
Beginner*

Finished Size
Approximately 40 x 40 inches

Materials
- Coats & Clark Red Heart Baby Sport Econo Pompadour 90 percent acrylic/10 percent olefin yarn (480 yds/6 oz per skein): 3 skeins candy print #1047
- Size 6 (4mm) needles or size needed to obtain gauge
- Tapestry needle
- Size G/6 (4mm) crochet hook

Gauge
20 sts and 27 rows = 4 inches/10cm in St st

To save time, take time to check gauge. ◆

Pattern Stitch
(Multiple of 20 sts + 2)

Rows 1, 3, 5, 7, 9 and 11 (RS): P1, *[k2, p2] twice, k2, [p1, k1] 5 times, rep from *, end p1.

Rows 2, 4, 6, 8, 10 and 12: K1, *[k1, p1] 5 times, [p2, k2] twice, p2, rep from *, end k1.

Rows 13, 15, 17, 19, 21 and 23: P1, *[k1, p1] 5 times, [k2, p2] twice, k2, rep from *, end p1.

Rows 14, 16, 18, 20, 22 and 24: K1, *[p2, k2] twice, p2, [p1, k1] 5 times, rep from *, end k1.

Rep Rows 1–24 for patt.

Afghan Strips
Make 4

CO 62 sts. Work in patt until piece meas 40 inches. BO loosely.

Finishing
Sew strips side by side. Crochet 1 rnd of sc around edges. Turn and work rnd of reverse sc (crab stitch) around. Fasten off. ❖

Blocks & Bars Mosaic Afghan

Design by E. J. Slayton

Create a cozy throw or afghan with handy take-along strips. The mosaic pattern is worked in one color at a time.

Experience Level
Intermediate***

Afghan

Finished Size
Approximately 30 x 48(36 x 60)(42 x 72) inches Instructions are given for smallest size, with larger sizes in parentheses. When only 1 number is given, it applies to all sizes.

Materials
- Brown Sheep Company's Cotton Fleece (80 percent pima cotton/20 percent merino wool, 215 yds/100g per skein): 5(6)(9) skeins lapis #CW-590 (MC), 4(5)(7) skeins Provencal rose #CW-220 (CC)
- Size 6 (4mm) needles or size needed to obtain gauge
- Tapestry needle

Gauge
24 sts and 50 rows = 4 inches/ 10cm in mosaic patt

To save time, take time to check gauge.

Pattern Notes
Sl all sts purlwise with yarn on WS of fabric; in back on RS rows, in front on WS rows.

Mosaic knitting creates color patterns, while working with only 1 color at a time. Stitches of the other color are slipped from the previous row, which also gives the fabric a thermal quality.

Pattern Stitch
Blocks & Bars Mosaic
(Multiple of 12 sts + 9)

Row 1(RS): With CC, [k1, sl 1] 4 times, *k5, sl 1, [k1, sl 1] 3 times, rep from * to last st, end k1.

Row 2: With CC, rep Row 1.

Row 3: With MC, k2, [sl 1, k1] twice, sl 1, *k7, sl 1, [k1, sl 1] twice, rep from * to last 2 sts, end k2.

Row 4: With MC, k1, p1, sl 1, [p1, sl 1] twice, *p7, sl 1, [p1, sl 1] twice, rep from * to last 2 sts, end p1, k1.

Rows 5–8: Rep Rows 1–4.

Rows 9 and 10: Rep Rows 1 and 2.

Row 11: With MC, knit.

Row 12: With MC, k1, p to last st, k1.

Rows 13 and 14: With CC, k1, sl 1, k5, *sl 1, [k1, sl 1] 3 times, k5, rep from * to last 2 sts, end sl 1, k1.

Row 15: With MC, k8, *sl 1, [k1, sl 1] twice, k7, rep from * to last st, end k1.

Row 16: With MC, k1, p7, *sl 1, [p1, sl 1] twice, p7, rep from * to last st, end k1.

Rows 17–20: Rep Rows 13–16.

Rows 21 and 22: Rep Rows 13 and 14.

Rows 23 and 24: Rep Rows 11 and 12.

Rep Rows 1–24 for patt.

Right Panel
With MC, CO 52(62)(72) sts.

Beg with a WS row, work 4 ridges of garter st, dec 1 st at beg of next and every RS row 3 times. (49, 59, 69 sts)

Inc row (RS): Inc 8(10)(12) sts evenly across. (57, 69, 81 sts)

Next row: Purl across. Beg with Row 1, work [Rows 1–24] 18(23)(28) times.

Dec row (RS): Knit across, dec 8(10)(12) sts evenly across (49, 59, 69 sts)

Knit 6 rows (3 ridges), inc 1 st at beg of each RS row. (52, 62, 72 sts)

BO all sts knitwise on WS.

Left Panel
Work as for right panel, working shaping at end of RS rows.

Center Panel

With MC, CO 49(59)(69) sts and work as for right panel, omitting corner shaping in borders, beg patt with Row 13 and ending with Row 12.

Finishing

With MC and RS facing, pick up and k 1 st for every 2 rows along edge of side panel that has mitered corner.

Work in garter st as for ends, inc 1 st at each end [every RS row] 3 times. (3 ridges)

BO all sts knitwise on WS. Rep for other side.

Sew corner seams. Join panels, working bet first and second sts from edges of panels. This will make a line of 2 MC sts. Block lightly.

Pillow

Finished Size

To fit 18-inch-square pillow

Materials

- Brown Sheep Company's Cotton Fleece (80 percent pima cotton/20 percent merino wool, 215 yds/100g per skein): 1 skein lapis #CW-590 (MC), 1 skein Provencal rose #CW-220 (CC)
- Size 6 (4mm) needles or size needed to obtain gauge
- Tapestry needle
- Covered 18-inch-square pillow
- Sewing needle and thread

Gauge

24 sts and 50 rows = 4 inches/10cm in mosaic patt (before blocking)

To save time, take time to check gauge.

Pattern Note

Knitted piece is stretched to fit pillow and sewn in place around edges.

To cover both sides of pillow, you will need an additional skein of MC.

Pattern Stitch

Blocks & Bars Mosaic

(Multiple of 12 sts + 3)

Row 1(RS): With CC, k1, sl 1, *k5, sl 1, [k1, sl 1] 3 times, rep from * to last st, end k1.

Row 2: With CC, rep Row 1.

Row 3: With MC, k1, *k7, sl 1, [k1, sl 1] twice, rep from * to last 2 sts, end k2.

Row 4: With MC, k1, p1, *sl 1, [p1, sl 1] twice, p7, rep from * to last st, end k1.

Rows 5–8: Rep Rows 1–4.

Rows 9 and 10: Rep Rows 1 and 2.

Row 11: With MC, knit.

Row 12: With MC, k1, p to last st, k1.

Row 13: With CC, k1, sl 1, *[k1, sl 1] 3 times, k5, sl 1, rep from * to last st, end k1.

Row 14: With CC, k1, sl 1, *k5, [sl 1, k1] 3 times, sl 1, rep from * to last st, end k1.

Row 15: With MC, k2, *sl 1, [k1, sl 1] twice, k7, rep from * to last st, end k1.

Row 16: With MC, k1, *p7, sl 1, [p1, sl 1] twice, rep from * to last 2 sts, end k2.

Rows 17–20: Rep Rows 13–16.

Rows 21 and 22: Rep Rows 13 and 14.

Rows 23 and 24: Rep Rows 11 and 12.

Rep Rows 1–24 for patt.

With MC, CO 69 sts.

Beg with a WS row, work 4 ridges of garter st, dec 1 st at each end [every RS row] 3 times and ending with a WS row. (63 sts)

Inc row: Knit, inc 12 sts evenly across. (75 sts)

Work patt [Rows 1–24] 5 times, then rep Rows 1–12.

Dec row: Knit, dec 12 sts evenly across. (63 sts)

Knit 6 rows (3 ridges), inc 1 st at each end of each RS row. BO all sts knitwise on WS.

Finishing

With MC and RS facing, pick up and k 1 st for every 2 rows along edge.

Work in garter st as for ends, inc 1 st at each end [every RS row] 3 times. (3 ridges)

BO all sts knitwise. Rep for other side.

Sew corners.

Pin knitted piece evenly to top of pillow and sew in place. ❖

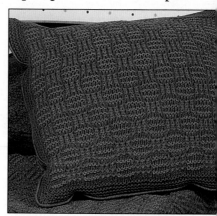

Elizabeth's Squares

Design by Diane Zangl

The basic square for this afghan was created for Elizabeth Zimmermann's 80th birthday afghan. It was inspired by the traditional Log Cabin quilt pattern of early America.

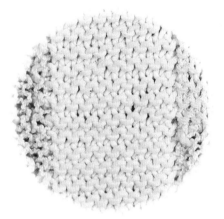

Experience Level
Advanced****

Finished Size
Approximately 41 x 50(50 x 64) inches. Instructions are given for throw, with afghan in parentheses. When only 1 number is given, it applies to both sizes.

Materials
- JCA/Reynolds Inc. Tucson worsted weight 65 percent cotton/35 percent acrylic yarn (118 yds/50g per ball): 9(14) balls natural #04 (A)
- JCA/Reynolds Inc. Serenity worsted weight bouclé cotton yarn (102 yds/50 per ball): 6(9) balls natural #700 (B)
- JCA/Reynolds Inc. Cantata worsted weight 90 percent cotton/10 percent nylon yarn (110 yds/50g per ball): 4(6) balls natural #101 (C)
- JCA/Reynolds Inc. Tiara worsted weight 70 percent viscose/30 percent silk yarn (109 yds/50g per ball): 2(3) balls ecru #01(D)
- Size 6 (4mm) needles or size needed to obtain gauge
- Tapestry needle

Gauge
18 sts and 36 rows (18 ridges) = 4 inches/10cm in garter stitch

To save time, take time to check gauge.

Pattern Notes
Basic piece is worked entirely in garter stitch, giving a square gauge. Square starts at outside edges and is worked inward (see Fig. 1 on page 128). Short rows and saddling techniques are used to achieve color changes.

Make 20 squares for throw, 30 squares for afghan. Pillow is one larger square.

Special Abbreviations
Make 1 left (M1L): Make a clockwise loop and place on RH ndl.

Make 1 right (M1L): Make a counterclockwise loop and place on RH ndl.

Afghan

Afghan Square

Make 20(30)

Section 1
With color A, CO 40 sts. Work even in garter st for 20 rows ending with a WS row. (10 ridges)

Next row: K10, turn. Work even on these 10 sts only for 30 more ridges. (40 ridges total along right edge of square)

Piece will look like a backwards "L". BO, leaving last lp on RH ndl. Cut A, change to color B.

Section 2
Referring to Fig. 1, pick up and k 29 sts along edge of narrow section just completed. (30 sts)

FIG. 1

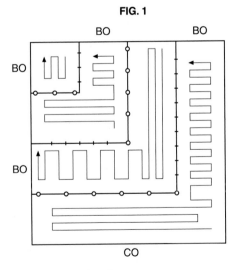

Sequence of work

CO, *work across all sts, then up right side for chosen width and length, give piece a quarter turn clockwise, work across all sts, then work up narrow side for chosen width, give piece a quarter turn counterclockwise and repeat from *. Sections are joined by means of picking up sts and k2tog.

Pick up last ridge st and place on LH ndl. (31 sts)

[K2tog, turn, sl 1 wyib, k to end of row, turn, k30] 10 times. (10 ridges of color B)

Next row: [K2tog, turn, sl 1 wyib, k10, turn, k10] 20 times. End with a RS row. BO color B. Cut yarn and fasten off last st. Change to color C.

Section 3

Beg at inside corner with RS facing, pick up and k 21 sts along edge of narrow section just completed. K20 [k2tog, turn, sl 1 wyib, k to end of row, turn, k20] 9 times. (10 ridges of color C)

[K2tog, turn, sl 1 wyib, k10, turn, k10] 10 times. BO, leaving last lp on RH ndl. Cut yarn, change to color D.

Section 4

Pick up and k 9 sts along edge of narrow section just completed. (10 sts)

Pick up last ridge st and place on LH ndl. [K2tog, turn, sl 1 wyib, k to end of row, turn, k10] 10 times. End with a WS row. BO rem sts.

Finishing

Sew squares tog in desired arrangement (see Fig. 2). For throw there are 5 rows of 4 squares each; afghan has 6 rows of 5 squares each.

Border

Long Edge

With circular ndls and color B, pick up and k 200(240) sts along 1 long edge. *Work in garter st for 6 rows, inc 1 st each end eor.*

Change to color C and rep from * to *.

Change to color D and rep from * to *.

Change to color A and rep

from * to *, working 8 rows instead of 6. BO all sts, leaving an 18-inch end for sewing. Rep for rem long edge.

Short Edge

Pick up and k160(200) sts along short end of afghan. Work as for long edge. Rep for rem edge.

Sew corner seams. Block.

Pillow

Finished Size

14 inches square, without border

Materials

- JCA/Reynolds Inc. Tucson worsted weight 65 percent cotton/35 percent acrylic yarn (118 yds/50g per ball): 1 ball natural #04 (A)
- JCA/Reynolds Inc. Serenity worsted weight bouclé cotton yarn (102 yds/50g per ball): 1 ball natural #700 (B)
- JCA/Reynolds Inc. Cantata worsted weight 90 percent cotton/10 percent nylon yarn (110 yds/50g per ball): 1 ball natural #101 (C)
- JCA/Reynolds Inc. Tiara worsted weight 70 percent viscose/30 percent silk yarn (109 yds/50g per ball): 1 ball ecru #01(D)
- Size 6 (4mm) straight and 24-inch circular needles or size needed to obtain gauge
- Tapestry needle
- 14-inch-square pillow form

Gauge

18 sts and 36 rows (18 ridges) = 4 inches/10cm in garter stitch

To save time, take time to check gauge.

Section 1

With color A, CO 56 sts. Work even in garter st for 28 rows ending with a WS row. (14 ridges)

Next row: K14, turn. Work even on these 14 sts only for 42 more ridges. (56 ridges total along right edge of square)

Piece will look like a backwards "L". BO, leaving last lp on RH ndl. Cut yarn, change to color B.

Section 2

Referring to Fig. 1, pick up and k 41 sts along edge of narrow section just completed. (42 sts)

Pick up last ridge st and place on LH ndl. (43 sts)

[K2tog, turn, sl 1 wyib, k to end of row, turn, k42] 14 times. There are 14 ridges of color B.

Next row: [K2tog, turn, sl 1

FIG. 2

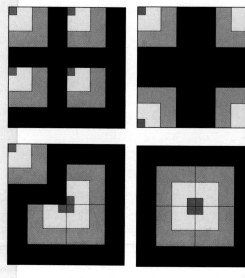

VARIATIONS ON PLACEMENT

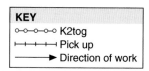

wyib, k14, turn, k14] 28 times. End with a RS row. BO color B. Cut yarn and fasten off last st. Change to color C.

Section 3

Beg at inside corner with RS facing, pick up and k 29 sts along edge of narrow section just completed. K28 [k2tog, turn, sl 1 wyib, k to end of row, turn, k28] 13 times. (14 ridges of color C)

[K2tog, turn, sl 1 wyib, k14, turn, k14] 14 times. BO, leaving last lp on RH ndl. Cut yarn,

change to color D.

Section 4

Pick up and k 13 sts along edge of narrow section just completed. (14 sts)

Pick up last ridge st and place on LH ndl. [K2tog, turn, sl 1 wyib, k to end of row, turn, k14] 14 times. End with WS row. BO rem sts.

Finishing

Pillow Border

With circular ndl and color D,

[pick up and k 56 sts along one side, pick up and k 1 st in corner, mark this st] 4 times. (228 sts)

Join and work in rnds.

Rnd 1: [P to marker, k 1] 4 times.

Rnd 2: [K to marker, M1L, k marked st, M1R] 4 times.

[Rep Rows 1 and 2] once, then [rep Rnd 1] once. (3 ridges)

BO all sts knitwise.

Sew pillow top to pillow form. ❖

Medallion Check

Design by Lois S. Young

This beautiful lace pattern is worth the extra effort!
It's worked in squares, so it's very portable.

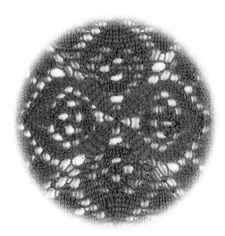

Experience Level
Advanced****

Finished Measurements
Approximately 50 x 66 inches

Materials
- Dale of Norway 100 percent wool sport weight yarn (108yds/50g per skein): 26 skeins teal #6135
- Size 5 (3.75 mm) set of 5 double-pointed and 16-inch circular needles or size needed to obtain gauge
- Size 6 (4mm) or size needed to obtain gauge
- Stitch markers
- Tapestry needle

Gauge
14 sts = 4 inches/10cm in lace patt with smaller ndls (blocked)

18 sts and 36 rows = 4 inches/10cm in garter st with larger ndls (blocked)

To save time, take time to check gauge.

Pattern Notes
On garter st squares, sl first st of each row purlwise.

Lace squares are worked from center out in 4 identical sections.

Even numbered rnds are worked as knit, except for second loop of a double yo, which is worked as purl.

Beg lace square by CO sts evenly divided onto 2 dpns. Change to 4 dpns on Rnd 7 and circular ndl on Rnd 15, pM bet reps.

Lace must be stretched severely to achieve its open pattern. Dampen and pin out to 8½-inch square. When pins are removed after drying, piece will relax to 8-inch square.

Garter Stitch Squares
With larger ndls, CO 35 sts. Work 69 rows [sl 1, k to end of row]. BO all sts knitwise. (35 ridges)

Lace Squares
Wrap yarn in ½-inch circle twice, leaving 2-inch tail, then using 2 dpns, CO 4 sts on each ndl by *picking up and k 1 st from under circle of yarn, yo, rep from *. (8 sts) K 1 rnd, pM for beg of rnd bet first and 2nd st. Pull on tail from circle to close center.

Work Rnds 1–24 from Chart A. BO loosely in purl. Dampen square and pin out, stretching severely, to 8½-inch square. Let dry.

STITCH KEY
☐	K on RS, p on WS
⊟	P on RS, k on WS
⊙	Yo
●⊙	Double yo; on next rnd, k1 in first loop, p1 in second loop
╱	K2tog
╲	Ssk
⅄	Sl1, k2tog, pass 2 sl sts over k2tog
ℛ	K1b
⍵	K1, yo, k1 in same st
▨	No st
⋒	Sl1
▬	Bo

CHART B

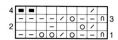

CHART A

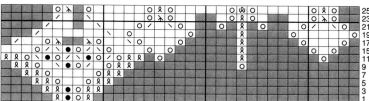

Note: Chart shows only odd-numbered rnds. On even-numbered rnds, knit, except on double-yo's, p1 in second loop.

Afghan

Make 24 garter st squares and 24 lace squares. Sew squares tog in checkerboard style to form a rectangle 6 squares wide and 8 squares long.

Edging

(Make 2 long and 2 short strips)

With larger ndls, CO 7 sts. Work 13 rows sl 1, k6. Beg Chart B. Rep Rows 1–4 from Chart B until lace portion meas same length as edge of afghan. BO after Row 4 (WS).

Sew edging to sides of afghan so there is a garter st square of edging at each corner of afghan. Sew ends of edging tog. ❖

Golden Ferns Counterpane

Design by Dawn Brocco

Knit this timeless classic with its touch of romance. The blocks are worked diagonally from corner to corner.

Experience Level
Intermediate***

Finished Size
Afghan: 44 x 58 inches (excluding edging)
Pillow: 14 inches square

Materials
- Brown Sheep Co. Lamb's Pride Worsted 85 percent wool/15 percent mohair (190 yds/113g per skein): 16 skeins imperial yellow #M-125
- Size 8 (5mm) double-pointed and 29-inch circular needles or size needed to obtain gauge
- Size G/6 (4mm) crochet hook
- Tapestry needle
- 14-inch-square covered pillow form

Gauge
18 sts and 26 rows = 4 inches/10cm in St st

To save time, take time to check gauge.

Pattern Note
Blocks beg at one corner and are worked diagonally across to opposite corner.

Special Abbreviation
Make 1 (M1): Inc by making a backward loop over right ndl.

Pattern Stitch
Seed Stitch (odd number of sts)

Row 1: K1, *p1, k1, rep from * across.

Rep Row 1 for patt.

Block
CO 3 sts.

Row 1 and odd-numbered rows through Row 35 (WS): Purl.

Row 2: M1, k3, M1. (5 sts)

Row 4: M1, k2tog, yo, k1, yo, ssk, M1. (7 sts)

Row 6: M1, k2tog, k1, yo, k1, yo, k1, ssk, M1. (9 sts)

Row 8: M1, k2tog, k2, yo, k1, yo, k2, ssk, M1. (11 sts)

Row 10: M1, k2tog, k3, yo, k1, yo, k3, ssk, M1. (13 sts)

Row 12: M1, [k1, yo] twice, ssk, k5, k2tog, [yo, k1] twice, M1. (17 sts)

Row 14: M1, k2tog, [k1, yo] twice, k1, ssk, k3, k2tog, [k1, yo] twice, k1, ssk, M1. (19 sts)

Row 16: M1, k2tog, k2, yo, k1, yo, k2, ssk, k1, k2tog, k2, yo, k1, yo, k2, ssk, M1. (21 sts)

Row 18: M1, k2tog, k3, yo, k1, yo, k3, sl 1, k2tog, psso, k3, yo, k1, yo, k3, ssk, M1. (23 sts)

Row 20: M1, [k1, yo] twice, ssk, k5, k2tog, yo, k1, yo, ssk, k5, k2tog, [yo, k1] twice, M1. (27 sts)

Row 22: M1, k2tog, [{k1, yo} twice, k1, ssk, k3, k2tog] twice [k1, yo] twice, k1, ssk, M1. (29 sts)

Row 24: M1, k2tog, [k2, yo, k1, yo, k2, ssk, k1, k2tog] twice, k2, yo, k1, yo, k2, ssk, M1. (31 sts)

Row 26: M1, k2tog, [k3, yo, k1, yo, k3, sl 1, k2tog, psso] twice, k3, yo, k1, yo, k3, ssk, M1. (33 sts)

Row 28: M1, [k1, yo] twice, [ssk, k5, k2tog, yo, k1, yo] 3 times, k1, M1. (37 sts)

Row 30: M1, k2tog, [{k1, yo} twice, k1, ssk, k3, k2tog] 3 times, [k1, yo] twice, k1, ssk, M1. (39 sts)

Row 32: M1, k2tog, [k2, yo, k1, yo, k2, ssk, k1, k2tog] 3 times, k2, yo, k1, yo, k2, ssk, M1. (41 sts)

Row 34: M1, k2tog, [k3, yo, k1, yo, k3, sl 1, k2tog, psso] 3 times, k3, yo, k1, yo, k3, ssk, M1. (43 sts)

Row 36: Ssk, p to last 2 sts, k2tog. (41 sts)

Row 37: Purl across.

Row 38: Ssk, work seed st to last 2 sts, k2tog. (39 sts)

Row 39: P1, work seed st to last st, p1.

Row 40: Rep Row 38. (37 sts)

Row 41: Rep Row 39.

Row 42: Ssk, k to last 2 sts, k2tog. (35 sts)

Row 43: P1, k to last st, p1.

Row 44: Ssk, k to last 2 sts, k2tog. (33 sts)

Row 45: Purl across.

Row 46: Ssk, purl to last 2 sts, k2tog. (31 sts)

Row 47: P1, knit to last st, p1.

Row 48: Rep Row 44. (29 sts)

Row 49: Rep Row 45.

Row 50: Ssk, p to last 2 sts, k2tog. (27 sts)

Row 51: Purl across.

Row 52: Ssk, work seed st to last 2 sts, k2tog. (25 sts)

Row 53: P1, work seed st to last st, p1.

Row 54: Rep Row 52. (23 sts)

Row 55: Rep Row 53.

Row 56: Ssk, k to last 2 sts, k2tog. (21 sts)

Row 57: P1, knit to last st, p1.

Row 58: Ssk, p6, k2tog, yo, k1, yo, ssk, p6, k2tog. (19 sts)

Row 59: P1, k6, p5, k6, p1.

Row 60: Ssk, p4, k2tog, [k1, yo] twice, k1, ssk, p4, k2tog. (17 sts)

Row 61: P1, k4, p7, k4, p1.

Row 62: Ssk, p2, k2tog, k2, yo, k1, yo, k2, ssk, p2, k2tog. (15 sts)

Row 63: P1, k2, p9, k2, p1.

CHART A

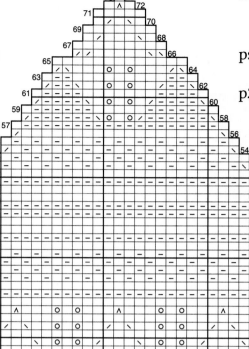

STITCH KEY
- ☐ K on RS, p on WS
- ⊟ P on RS, k on WS
- Ⓜ M1
- ☑ K2tog
- ◺ Ssk
- ⊙ Yo
- ◭ Sl1, k2tog, psso
- ◮ Sl2tog tbl, p1, p2sso

Row 64: Ssk, k2tog, k3, yo, k1, yo, k3, ssk, k2tog. (13 sts)

Row 65: Purl across.

Row 66: [Ssk] twice, k5, [k2tog] twice. (9 sts)

Row 67: Purl across.

Row 68: K1, ssk, k3, k2tog, k1. (7 sts)

Row 69: Purl across.

Row 70: K1, ssk, k1, k2tog, k1. (5 sts)

Row 71: Purl across.

Row 72: K1, sl 1, k2tog, psso, k1. (3 sts)

Row 73: Sl 2 tog tbl, p1, p2sso. Fasten off last st.

Make 52 squares, following written directions or Chart A.

Afghan

Place groups of 4 squares tog, with single leaf motifs in center. With RS tog, using crochet hook and yarn, sl st squares tog. (13 blocks)

Reserving 1 block for pillow, [sl st 3 blocks tog in a panel] 4 times. Sl st panels tog for afghan. (3 blocks x 4 blocks)

Edging

With RS facing, using circular ndl, pick up and k 33 sts along edge of each square across a short side. (198 sts)

Row 1 (WS): Knit.

Row 2 (RS): Knit.

Row 3: Purl.

Row 4: With a separate ndl, ssk, p29, k2tog. (31 sts)

Leave rem sts on circular ndl, turn.

Row 5: P2tog, k27, p2tog tbl. (29 sts)

Row 6: Ssk, k25, k2tog. (27 sts)

Row 7: P2tog, p23, p2tog tbl. (25 sts)

Row 8: Ssk, p21, k2tog. (23 sts)

Row 9: P2tog, k19, p2tog tbl. (21 sts)

Continued on page 141

Around the World Afghan & Pillow

Design by Laura Polley

Use yarn from other projects for the random-colored blocks to knit an afghan full of memories. Simple garter stitch creates this traditional quilt pattern.

Experience Level
Intermediate***

Finished Size
Approximately 52 x 64 inches, including border (in twisted garter st) or 52 x 79 inches including border (in regular garter st)

Materials
- Coats & Clark Red Heart TLC 100 percent acrylic worsted weight yarn (253 yds/5 oz per skein): 9 skeins natural #5017 (MC), 4 skeins navy #5861 (A), 1 skein each of CC's: claret #5915, royal blue #5885, light purple #5587, dark purple #5595, fuchsia #5768, dark sage #5666, cherry red #5911, dark teal #5809, cognac #5288, red #5900, emerald #5687, forest green #5690
- Size 9 (5.5mm) needles or size needed to obtain gauge.
- 2 size 9 (5.5mm) circular needles, 29-inches or longer (for pillow)
- 14-inch pillow form
- Tapestry needle

Gauge
20 sts and 32 rows = 4 inches/10cm in twisted garter st or

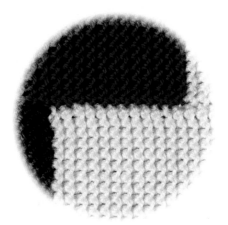

16 sts and 32 rows = 4 inches/10cm in garter st

To save time, take time to check gauge.

Pattern Notes
Patt is written for twisted garter st, with changes for regular garter st in parentheses.

Projects may be worked in either technique, but be sure to use same technique throughout project. Afghan is shown in twisted garter st. Pillow is shown in regular garter st. Pillow size is same for both techniques. Yarn amounts will be sufficient for either technique.

Work in ends as you go by catching them over and under working yarn for approximately 2 inches.

When working color blocks, choose colors at random. More or fewer colors may be used if desired. Color A (navy) is used as a CC within afghan and pillow as well as for borders.

Afghan and pillow are

worked from side-to-side. Garter stitch ridges will be vertical when assembled correctly.

Pattern Stitches
Garter St: Knit every row.

Twisted Garter St: Knit every row, working all sts tbl.

Afghan
Work strips as indicated below.

Strip A
Make 4

(CC half blocks at beg and end)

With CC of your choice, CO 20 sts. K 24 rows, [k 48 rows MC, k 48 rows in desired CC] 3 times, k 48 rows MC, k 24 rows CC. BO all sts. (384 rows)

Strip B
Make 3

(MC half blocks at beg and end)

With MC, CO 20 sts. K 24 rows, [k 48 rows CC, k 48 rows MC] 3 times, k 48 rows CC, k 24 rows MC. BO all sts. (384 rows)

Strip C
Make 4

(Beg with full CC block)

With CC of your choice, CO 20 sts. [K 48 rows CC, k 48 rows MC] twice, then [k 48 rows MC, k 48 rows CC] twice. BO all sts. (384 rows)

Strip D
Make 4

(Beg with full MC block)

With MC, CO 20 sts. [K 48 rows MC, k 48 rows CC] twice, then [k 48 rows CC, k 48 rows MC] twice. BO. (384 rows)

Assembly

Arrange strips in following sequence: C, A, D, B, C, A, D, B, D, A, C, B, D, A, C. Sew strips tog.

Border

With A, CO 10 sts. *K 384 rows.

Beg corner patt

Row 1 (RS): Knit to end.

Row 2 (WS): K9, turn.

Rows 3, 5, 7, 9, 11 and 13: Sl 1 purlwise wyib, k to end.

Row 4: K8, turn.

Row 6: K7, turn.

Row 8: K6, turn.

Row 10: K5, turn.

Row 12: K3, turn.

Row 14: K1, turn.

Row 15: K1.

Row 16: (WS): K10.

Rows 17–32: Rep Rows 1–16.

When Rows 1–32 of corner patt are completed, k 480(600) rows, [work Rows 1–32 of corner patt] once, [rep from *] once. BO all sts. Sew CO and BO edges of border tog.

Finishing

Pin border to afghan and sew in place using A.

For textured garter st afghan

Match ridge to ridge when sewing border to row ends (top and bottom edges). When sewing border to CO and BO edges of afghan (side edges), sew 16 ridges of border to every 20 sts (one color-block width.)

For garter st afghan

Match ridge for ridge along row ends (top and bottom edges) and sew one ridge to each st along CO and BO edges (side edges).

Block if desired.

Pillow

Finished Size

14 inches square

Back

With A, CO 70(56) sts. Knit 112 rows. BO all sts.

Front

Work strips as indicated below.

Strip A

Make 2

With MC, CO 10(8) sts. K 112 rows. BO all sts.

Strip B

Make 2

With MC, CO 10(8) sts. K 42 rows. With CC, k 28 rows. With MC, k 42 rows. BO all sts. (112 rows)

Strip C

Make 2

With MC, CO 10(8) sts. With MC, k 28 rows. With CC, k 28 rows. With a different CC, k 28 rows. With MC, k 28 rows. BO all sts. (112 rows)

Strip D

Make 2

With MC, CO 10(8) sts. K 14 rows. With CC, k 28 rows. With MC, k 28 rows. With CC, k 28 rows. With MC, k 14 rows. BO all sts. (112 rows)

Assembly

Arrange strips in following sequence: A, B, C, D, C, B, A.

With RS facing, sew strips tog.

Join front and back

With RS facing, using circular ndl and A, pick up and k 56 sts along each side edge of pillow. Do not join. (224 total sts around pillow)

Set aside. Rep on rem piece, using second circular ndl.

Holding pieces with WS tog, pillow front facing, and pillow form in bet pieces, line up last sts of front and back pick-up rows.

BO front and back sts tog as follows:

Hold ndls containing sts parallel, right sides tog; with 3rd ndl, k first st on front and back ndls tog, *k next st on both ndls tog, BO 1, rep from * until all sts are worked, fasten off. ❖

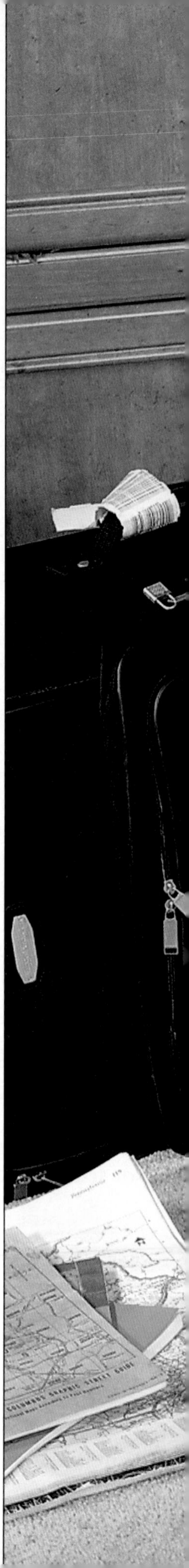

Kaleidoscope of Leaves Afghan

Design by Nazanin S. Fard

Knit this challenging afghan one block at a time.
Blocks are knit diagonally from corner to corner.

Experience Level
Advanced****

Finished Measurements
Approximately 66 x 66 inches

Materials
- Coats & Clark Red Heart Super Saver 100 percent acrylic worsted weight yarn (452 yds/8 oz per skein): 6 skeins light grey #341
- Size 8 (5mm) needles or size needed to obtain gauge
- Cable needle
- Size G/6 (4mm) crochet hook
- Fairfield Processing Co. 12-inch-square pillow form
- 25 x 13-inch piece gray fabric

Gauge
20 sts and 8 rows = 4 inches/ 10cm in St st

To save time, take time to check gauge.

Pattern Note
Blocks beg at 1 corner and are worked diagonally across to opposite corner.

Special Abbreviations
Cable 1 left (C1L): Sl next st to cn, hold in front, p1, k1 from cn.

Cable 1 right (C1R): Sl next st to cn, hold in back, k1, p1, from cn.

Inc 1: P in front and back of same st.

Make 1 (M1): Inc 1 st by knitting in front and back of same st.

Twist 1 left (T1L): With RH ndl in back of LH ndl, k1b in second st on LH ndl, leave on ndl, k1 in front lp of first st, sl both sts off ndl tog.

Afghan
Block
CO 3 sts.

Row 1 (RS): Purl.

Row 2: K1, k in [front, back, front] of same st, k1. (5 sts)

Row 3: P2, k1, p2.

Row 4: K1, M1, p1, M1, k1. (7 sts)

Row 5: P3, k1, p3.

Row 6: K1, M1, k1, p1, k1, M1, k1. (9 sts)

Row 7: P3, k3, p3.

Row 8: K1, M1, k1, p3, k1, M1, k1. (11 sts)

Row 9: P3, C1R, k1, C1L, p3.

Row 10: K1, M1, [k1, p1] 3 times, k1, M1, k1.

Row 11: P3, C1R, p1, k1, p1, C1L, p3.

Row 12: K1, M1, k1, [p1, k2] twice, p1, k1, M1, k1. (15 sts)

Row 13: P4, [k1, p2] twice, k1, p4.

Row 14: K1, M1, [k2, p1] 3 times, k2, M1, k1.

Row 15: P3, p2tog, [k1, yo, k1] in next st, inc 1, p1, k1, p1, inc 1, [k1, yo, k1] in next st, p2tog, p3.

Row 16: K1, M1, k2, p3, k3, p1, k3, p3, k2, M1, k1. (23 sts)

Row 17: P3, p2tog, [k1, yo] twice, k1, inc 1, p2, k1, p2, inc 1, [k1, yo] twice, k1, p2tog, p3. (27 sts)

Row 18: K1, M1, k2, p5, k4, p1, k4, p5, k2, M1, k1. (29 sts)

Row 19: P3, p2tog, k2, yo, k1, yo, k2, inc 1, p3, k1, p3, inc 1, k2, yo, k1, yo, k2, p2tog, p3. (33 sts)

Row 20: K1, M1, k2, p7, k5, p1, k5, p7, k2, M1, k1. (35 sts)

Row 21: P5, ssk, k3, k2tog, p5, (k1, yo, k1) in next st, p5, ssk, k3, k2tog, p5. (33 sts)

Row 22: K1, M1, k3, p5, k5, p3, k5, p5, k3, M1, k1. (35 sts)

Row 23: P6, ssk, k1, k2tog, p5, (k1, yo) twice, k1, p5, ssk, k1, k2tog, p6. (33 sts)

Row 24: K1, M1, k4, p3, k5, p5, k5, p3, k4, M1, k1. (35 sts)

Row 25: P7, k3tog, p5, k2, yo, k1, yo, k2, p5, k3tog, p7. (33 sts)

Row 26: K1, M1, k11, p7,

Row 37: K2, *yo, ssk, rep from *, end k1.

Row 38: P1, inc 1, p41, inc 1, p1. (47 sts)

Rows 39 and 41: Purl.

Row 40: K1, M1, k43, M1, k1. (49 sts)

Row 42: P1, ssp, p43, p2tog, p1. (47 sts)

Row 43: Rep Row 37.

Row 44: P1, ssp, p41, p2tog, p1. (45 sts)

Rows 45 and 47: Purl.

Row 46: K1, ssk, k39, k2tog, k1. (43 sts)

Row 48: K1, ssk, k37, k2tog, k1. (41 sts)

Row 49: P4, [T1L, p1] 11 times, end p4.

Row 50: K1, ssk, k2, [p2, k1] 11 times, end k2tog, k1. (39 sts)

Row 51: P3, [T1L, p1] 11 times, end p3.

Row 52: K1, ssk, [k1, p2] 11 times, end k2tog, k1. (37 sts)

Row 53: P2, [T1L, p1] 11 times, end p2.

Row 54: K1, ssk, k3, [p2, k1] 9 times, end k1, k2tog, k1. (35 sts)

Rows 55 and 57: P4, [T1L, p1] 9 times, end p4.

Row 56: K5, [p2, k1] 9 times, end k3. (35 sts)

Row 58: K1, ssk, k29, k2tog, k1. (33 sts)

Rows 59 and 61: Purl.

Row 60: K1, ssk, k27, k2tog, k1. (31 sts)

Row 62: K1, ssk, k25, k2tog, k1. (29 sts)

Row 63: P14, [k1, yo, k1] in next st, p14. (31 sts)

Row 64: K1, ssk, k11, p3, k11, k2tog, k1. (29 sts)

Row 65: P11, ssp, [k1, yo] twice, k1, p2tog, p11. (29 sts)

Row 66: K1, ssk, k9, p5, k9,

k11, M1, k1. (35 sts)

Row 27: P13, inc 1, k2tog, k3, ssk, inc 1, p13. (35 sts)

Row 28: K1, M1, k13, p5, k13, M1, k1. (37 sts)

Row 29: P15, inc 1, ssk, k1, k2tog, inc 1, p15.

Row 30: K1, M1, k15, p3, k15, M1, k1. (39 sts)

Row 31: P17, inc 1, k3tog, inc 1, p17.

Row 32: K1, M1, k35, M1, k1. (41 sts)

Rows 33 and 35: Purl.

Row 34: K1, M1, k37, M1, k1. (43 sts)

Row 36: P1, inc 1, p39, inc 1, p1. (45 sts)

Continued on page 141

Baby Blocks Blanket

Design by Edie Eckman

Here is a great baby afghan for a new knitter.

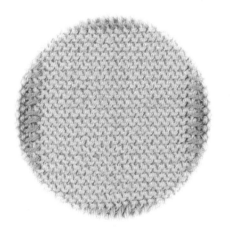

Experience Level
Beginner*

Finished Measurements
Approximately 29 x 37 inches

Materials
- Plymouth Yarn Co. Cleckheaton 8-ply 100 percent superwash wool worsted weight wool yarn from (106 yds/50g per ball): 6 balls pink #1840 (A), 4 balls green #1962 (B), 3 balls each blue #1935 (C), yellow #1939 (D)
- Size 7 (4.5mm) knitting needles

Pattern Note
Each skein of yarn makes exactly 5 squares. If you are making bigger squares or a larger blanket, purchase more yarn accordingly.

Gauge
18 sts and 36 rows (18 ridges) = 4 inches/10cm in garter st

To save time, take time to check gauge.

Square
Make 20 pink (A), 16 green (B), 15 blue (C), and 12 yellow (D)

CO 20 sts. Knit 40 rows (20 ridges). BO all sts.

Finishing
Arrange squares according to Fig. 1.

With A, whipstitch squares tog, whipstitch around outside edges. ❖

FIG. 1

⊲	B	⊲	B	⊲	B	⊲	B	⊲
C	◻	C	◻	C	◻	C	◻	C
⊲	B	⊲	B	⊲	B	⊲	B	⊲
C	◻	C	◻	C	◻	C	◻	C
⊲	B	⊲	B	⊲	B	⊲	B	⊲
C	◻	C	◻	C	◻	C	◻	C
⊲	B	⊲	B	⊲	B	⊲	B	⊲

Direction of letters indicates direction of ridges.

Malibu Chains Afghan

Continued from page 121

strip at a rate of 1 st in eor. Turn and k 1 row on WS, turn and work 4 rows of St st.

Make tuck

With WS facing, using smaller ndl, slide purl bumps of pick up row onto smaller ndl. Hold smaller and larger ndls tog and parallel. With B, k2 tog across [1 from thin needle and 1 from working needle] forming a tube.

Turn and knit 1 row on WS, placing markers for dec sections: k17, pM, [k16, pM] 4 times, end k17.

Dec row (RS): K1, [ssk, k to within 2 sts of marker, k2tog, sl marker] 5 times, end ssk, k to within 3 sts of end, k2tog, k1.

Golden Ferns Counterpane

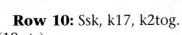

Continued from page 134

Row 10: Ssk, k17, k2tog. (19 sts)

Row 11: P2tog, p15, p2tog tbl. (17 sts)

Row 12: Ssk, p13, k2tog. (15 sts)

Row 13: P2tog, k11, p2tog tbl. (13 sts)

Row 14: Ssk, k9, k2tog. (11 sts)

Row 15: P2tog, p7, p2tog tbl. (9 sts)

Row 16: Ssk, p5, k2tog. (7 sts)

Row 17: P2tog, k3, p2tog tbl. (5 sts)

Row 18: Ssk, k1, k2tog. (3 sts)

WS row: Purl across.

Rep these 2 rows until 14 sts rem.

Next dec row: K1, [k2tog] 6 times, k1, turn.

Next row: P8, turn.

Next dec row: K1, [k2tog] 3 times, k1.

Cut yarn leaving a long tail. Thread tail through 5 rem sts, then use it to sew sides of panel tog, forming a circle. Rep for other end of bolster. Make 2 tassels as for afghan, reversing colors. Sew one tassel to each end at center of circle.

Finishing

Stuff fiberfill into bolster. Sew top and bottom of cable strips tog to close bolster. ❖

Row 19: Sl 2 tog tbl, p1, p2sso. (1 st)

Fasten off.

Rejoin yarn and rep Rows 4–19 for each 33 st section.

Rep for other short side of afghan.

For each long edge, work as above on 264 sts.

Pillow

With RS of rem block facing, pick up and k 33 sts along edge of each square. (66 sts)

Work edging as above on all sides.

Pillow Back

CO 64 sts. Work in St st for 14 inches. BO all sts.

Sew pillow front to back along 3 sides. Insert pillow form, sew last side. ❖

Kaleidoscope of Leaves Afghan

Continued from page 139

k2tog, k1. (27 sts)

Row 67: P9, ssp, k2, yo, k1, yo, k2, p2tog, p9.

Row 68: K1, ssk, k7, p7, k7, k2tog, k1. (25 sts)

Row 69: P9, ssk, k3, k2tog, p9. (23 sts)

Row 70: K1, ssk, k6, p5, k6, k2tog, k1. (21 sts)

Row 71: P8, ssk, k1, k2tog, p8. (19 sts)

Row 72: K1, ssk, k5, p3, k5, k2tog, k1. (17 sts)

Row 73: P7, k3tog, p7. (15 sts)

Row 74: K1, ssk, k3, k3tog, k3, k2tog, k1. (11 sts)

Row 75: P4, p3tog, p4. (9 sts)

Row 76: K1, ssk, k3, k2tog, k1. (7 sts)

Row 77: Purl.

Row 78: K1, ssk, k1, k2tog, k1. (5 sts)

Row 79: P1, p3tog, p1. (3 sts)

BO rem sts.

Make 36 blocks. Block each to size separately.

With crochet hook and WS tog, sc blocks tog in 6 rows of 6 blocks.

Finishing

With crochet hook, work 1 row of sc around afghan. Turn and work row of reverse sc around. Fasten off.

Pillow

Work 1 block as above, block it to size.

With crochet hook work 1 row of sc around afghan. Turn and work row of reverse sc around. Fasten off.

Finishing

Fold fabric in half. Sew 2 sides to make a pillow cover. Insert pillow form and stitch last side. Sew block to top of pillow. ❖

Spotlight on Sweaters

S *weaters are everywhere today. You see them on teenagers at school and on men and women at home and at work. You'll find summer tops, stylish vests, comfy tunics, classic pullovers and lovely cardigans in this chapter. There's a little bit of everything, so you can find just the right design to knit in your spare moments for just the right person.*

✈ Gate 5

Chapter 5

Strips of Lace Vest

Design by Joan McGowan

Three lace patterns worked separately in strips combine into a flattering vest.

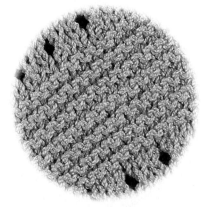

Experience Level
Intermediate***

Size
Women's small(medium) (large) Instructions are given for smallest size, with larger sizes in parentheses. When only 1 number is given, it applies to all sizes.

Finished Measurements
Chest: 30(34)(38)(42) inches

Length: 27(27)(28)(29) inches

Materials
• Smart Cotton worsted weight 68 percent cotton/29 percent rayon/3 percent nylon yarn from Berroco, Inc. (87 yds/50g per ball): 12(13)(13)(14) balls rose blush #1442
• Size 7 (4.5mm) needles or size needed to obtain gauge
• Tapestry needle

Gauge
18 sts and 26 rows = 4 inches/10cm in St st

To save time, take time to check gauge.

Special Abbreviation
Make 1 (M1): Pick up running thread bet sts without twisting, k1.

Strip A
Make 4

Fountain Lace
CO 17 sts.

Row 1 and rem WS rows: Purl.

Row 2: Ssk, yo, k2, k2tog, yo, k1, yo, k3tog, yo, k1, yo, ssk, k2, yo, k2tog.

Row 4: Ssk, k3, yo, k2tog, yo, k3, yo, ssk, yo, k3, k2tog.

Row 6: Ssk, [k2, yo] twice, k2tog, k1, ssk, [yo, k2] twice, k2tog.

Row 8: Ssk, k1, yo, k3, yo, k2tog, k1, ssk, yo, k3, yo, k1, k2tog.

Rep Rows 1–8 for patt until piece meas 26(27)(28)(29) inches from beg.

BO all sts.

Strip B
Make 2

Diagonal Eyelet
Rows 1–14: Knit.

Row 15: *K1, k2tog, yo, rep from * to last 2 sts, end k2tog.

Row 16: Purl.

Rep Rows 1–16 for patt.
CO 3 sts.

Knit 2 rows. Beg with Row 3, work in patt to last st, [M1, k1] every row until there are 20(25)(30)(35) sts on ndl.

Work even in est patt, k2tog at end of every RS row and M1 at end of every WS row until piece meas 17(19)(19)(20) inches from beg.

Shape underarm
Continue to work in est patt, dec 1 st at end of every row until 12(12)(13)(15) sts rem on ndl.

Work even until armhole meas 8(8)(8½)(9) inches from beg, then k2tog at end of every row until 1 st rem. Fasten off.

Strip C
Make 2

Work as B until there are 20(25)(30)(35) sts on ndl, then reverse shaping by M1 at end of every RS row and k2tog at end of every WS row.

Strip D
Make 1

CO 20 sts and knit 3 rows. Work even in Diagonal Eyelet patt by k2tog at end of every RS row and M1 at end of every WS row until piece meas 15(16)(17)(18) inches from beg.

Continue to work in est

Continued on page 167

Luscious Summer Cardigan

Design by Nazanin S. Fard

Modular construction makes for a truly knit-on-the-run project. Adjust the size by adding or omitting strips.

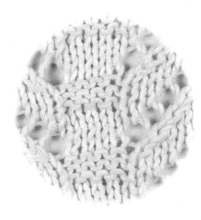

Experience Level
Intermediate***

Size
Women's medium

Finished Measurements
Chest: 42 inches
Armhole depth: 8 inches
Total length: 25 inches

Materials
- Naturally Cotton Connection D.K. No.7, 86 percent cotton/14 percent wool from S.R. Kertzer Ltd. (115 yds/50g per skein): 12 skeins beige #401
- Size 6 (4mm) needles or size needed to obtain gauge
- Cable needle
- Stitch holders
- Size C/2 (2.75mm) crochet hook
- 8 (¾-inch) buttons ivory #35488 from JHB International Inc.

Gauge
22 sts and 30 rows = 4 inches/ 10cm in moss st

To save time, take time to check gauge.

Pattern Notes
Beg each strip with 5 rows of garter st.

Size may be adjusted by adding or omitting strips of Patt A or moss st at underarm.

Pattern Stitches
Pattern A (panel of 18 sts)

Rows 1, 3 and 5 (WS): K2, p14, k2.

Row 2: P2, k3, k2tog, yo, k4, yo, ssk, k3, p2.

Row 4: P2, k2, k2tog, yo, k6, yo, ssk, k2, p2.

Row 6: P2, k1, k2tog, yo, k2, p4, k2, yo, ssk, k1, p2.

Row 7: K2, p5, k4, p5, k2.

Row 8: P2, k2tog, yo, k3, p4, k3, yo, ssk, p2.

Rep Rows 1–8 for patt.

Pattern B (panel of 9 sts)

Row 1 (WS): K3, p3, k3.

Row 2: P3, [k1, yo] twice, k1, p3. (11 sts)

Rows 3 and 9: K3, p5, k3.

Row 4: P3, k2, yo, k1, yo, k2, p3. (13 sts)

Rows 5 and 7: K3, p7, k3.

Row 6: P3, ssk, k1, [yo, k1] twice, k2tog, p3. (13 sts)

Row 8: P3, ssk, k3, k2tog, p3. (11 sts)

Row 10: P3, ssk, k1, k2tog, p3. (9 sts)

Row 11: K3, p3, k3.

Row 12: P3, yo, sl 2 tog knit-wise, k1, p2sso, yo, p3. (9 sts)

Rep Rows 1–12 for patt.

Pattern C (multiple of 10 sts) CO 7 sts.

Base Row 1 (WS): K2, p3, k2.

Base Row 2: P2, [k in front and back of same st] 3 times, p2. (10 sts)

Beg patt

Row 1 and rem WS rows: K2, p6, k2.

Row 2: P2, sl 3 sts on cn and hold in back, k3, k3 from cn, p2.

Rows 4, 6 and 8: P2, k6, p2.

Rep Rows 1–8 for patt.

Finishing row: P2, place 3 sts on cn and hold in back, [k 1 st from ndl and 1 st from cn tog] 3 times, p2. (7 sts rem)

Pattern D (even number of sts)

Row 1: * K1, p1, rep from * across.

Rows 2 and 4: K the knit sts and p the purl sts.

Row 3: *P1, k1, rep from * across.

Rep Rows 1–4 for patt.

Back
Work 4 strips patt A, and 2

Continued on page 168

Diagonal Delight

Design by Edie Eckman

Break out of the mold for neckline shaping with yarnovers and decreases, creating a diagonal fabric.

Experience Level
Advanced****

Size
Women's small(medium)(large)(extra-large)
Instructions are given for smallest size, with larger sizes in parentheses. When only 1 number is given it applies to all sizes.

Finished Measurements
Chest: 37(40)(42)(44) inches
Length: 21(22)(23)(23¾) inches

Materials
• JCA/Reynolds Inc. Saucy 100 percent cotton worsted weight yarn from JCA Inc. (185 yds/100g per ball): 5(6)(7)(8) balls
• Size 7 (4.5mm) 29-inch circular needle or size needed to obtain gauge
• Size G/6 (4mm) crochet hook
• Stitch holders
• Tapestry needle

Special Abbreviation
Make 1 (M1): Inc by making a backward loop over right ndl.

Gauge
20 sts and 28 rows = 4 inches/10cm in sleeve patt

To save time, take time to check gauge.

Pattern Notes
This patt is challenging because you must make decisions as you knit about how shaping is to be made. Instructions give guidelines, but it is up to you to determine best method of performing decs and incs in order to maintain proper stitch count.

Body is knit in 1 piece in rnds to underarms. This part is easy and allows you to become familiar with stitch patt and how it flows around garment. Once piece is divided for armholes it is worked back and forth, and this is where the fun starts. At that point, instructions will become somewhat narrative in order to allow you to make decisions about shaping.

Body
CO 187(198)(209)(220) sts (multiple of 11). Join without twisting, pM at beg of rnd.

Rnd 1: K1, *p6, yo, ssk, k3, rep from * around, end last rep k2.

Rnd 2: K1, *p6, k5, rep from * around, end last rep k4.

Rnds 3–8: [Rep Rnds 1 and 2] 3 times.

Rnd 9: *Ssk, k6, yo, k3, rep from * around.

Rnd 10: Knit.

Rep Rnds 9 and 10 for patt until piece meas 12(12¾)(13¼)(13¾) inches, ending with a knit rnd. (XL only: do not k last 2 sts of rnd)

Divide for front
Remove marker and cut yarn, leaving a tail for weaving. Sl next 4(8)(5)(2) sts onto RH ndl, then place last 94(99)(105)(110) sts worked onto holder for back. (93, 99, 104, 110 sts rem on ndl)

Armholes
***Note:** This sets up beg of armhole shaping so neck shaping will be in right place, but now it requires some thought on your part.*

So far, every yo inc has been accompanied by a ssk dec, so st count has rem constant. There are several ways to manage upcoming armhole decs, depending on which way dec slopes, and which size you are knitting. In all cases, selvage sts should remain in St st.

For left front armhole shaping, if you can stay in st patt but omit a yo, resulting ssk dec will create a left-sloping line. Therefore, as you look at front of your sweater, ready to knit, if a yo would ordinarily occur in patt within first 3 sts of row, just knit that st (no yo), then work ssk 3 sts later as it occurs in patt. However, if yo would not ordinarily occur until 4 or more sts

Continued on page 168

Patchwork Vest

Design by Yarn by Mills

Knit with two variegated yarns, no two vests will ever look alike.

Experience Level
Advanced beginner**

Size
Women's small(medium) (large) Instructions are given for smallest size, with larger sizes in parentheses. When only 1 number is given, it applies to all sizes.

Finished Measurements
Chest: 36(40)(44) inches
Length: 20(22)(22) inches

Materials
- Yarn by Mills 50 percent alpaca/50 percent wool worsted weight yarn (500 yds/8 oz per skein): 500 yds hand-dyed dark variegated (MC), 370 yds light variegated (CC)
- Size 8 (5mm) 16- and 24- or 29-inch circular needles or size needed to obtain gauge
- Stitch holders
- Stitch markers
- Tapestry needle

CHART A

CHART B

COLOR KEY
☐ MC
◇ CC

Rep

Gauge
18 sts and 19 rnds = 4 inches/ 10cm in color patt

To save time, take time to check gauge.

Pattern Note
Yarn amounts given are sufficient to complete all sizes.

Body
With longer circular ndl and MC, CO 162(180)(198) sts. Join without twisting and work in garter st (k 1 rnd, p 1 rnd) until piece meas 2 inches from beg.

Change to St st and work Rnds 1–8 from Chart A until piece meas 9 inches from beg.

Now work Rnds 1–6 from Chart B for 3½ inches, ending with Rnd 6. Rep Rnds 7–12 for rest of garment.

Front
At the same time, when body meas 12 inches from beg, work across first 81(90)(99) sts. Place rem 81(90)(99) sts on holder for back and work in rows on front sts, maintaining est patt throughout.

Shape armholes
BO 3 sts at beg of next 4 rows. (69, 78, 87 sts)

Work even in patt until piece meas 17(19)(19) inches from beg, ending with a WS row.

Shape front neck
Work across first 25(29)(32) sts, place center 19(20)(23) sts on holder for front neck and rem 25(29)(32) sts on another holder for right front.

Working on left front sts, purl 1 row. Continue in est patt, dec 1 st at neck edge [every RS row] 5 times, then work even on rem 20(24)(27) shoulder sts until piece meas 19½(21½)(21½) inches from beg, ending with a WS row.

Shape shoulder
At beg of next row, BO 10(12)(14) sts. Purl 1 row, then BO rem 10(12)(13) sts on next row.

Sl right front sts to ndl and complete as for left side, reversing shaping.

Back
Sl back sts to ndl and work armhole shaping as for front, then work even in patt until piece meas same as front to shoulders.

At beg of row, BO [10(12) (14) sts] twice, [10(12)(13) sts] twice, then BO rem 29(30)(33) sts for back neck.

Continued on page 171

Lilac Bouclé Sweater

Design by Laura Gebhardt

Here's a great quick-to-knit bulky for beginners to try.
It features a separate cowl to wear as you please.

Experience Level

Beginner*

Size

Women's small(medium)
(large)(extra-large)
Instructions are given for
smallest size, with larger
sizes in parentheses. When
only 1 number is given, it
applies to all sizes.

Finished Measurements

Chest: 40½(44¼)(48)(51½)
inches

Length: 23(25)(25)(26)
inches

Materials

- Melody 68 percent
  acrylic/32 percent nylon
  bulky weight yarn from
  Patons Inc. (85 yds/100g
  per ball): 5(5)(6)(7) balls
  lavender #907
- Size 15 (10mm) needles
  or size needed to obtain
  gauge
- Tapestry needle

Gauge

9 sts and 13 rows = 4 inch-
es/10cm in St st

To save time, take time to
check gauge.

Back

CO 46(50)(54)(58) sts.

Rows 1–10: Knit.

Work in St st until piece meas
22(24)(24)(25) inches from
beg, ending with a WS row.

Shape shoulders

K17(18)(20)(21), BO next
12(14)(14)(16) sts, k to end.

Working in St st on last
17(18)(20)(21) sts, dec 1 st at
neck edge [every row] twice,
then work 3 rows even. BO
rem 15(16)(18)(19) sts.

With WS facing, join yarn
at right neck edge and complete to match left side.

Front

Work as for back until piece
meas 20(22)(22)(23) inches
from beg.

Shape neck

K19(20)(22)(23), BO next
8(10)(10)(12) sts for front
neck, k to end.

Working in St st on last
19(20) (22)(23) sts, dec 1 st at
neck edge [every row] 4 times,
then work even on rem 15(16)
(18)(19) sts until front meas
same as back at shoulder. BO
all sts.

With WS facing, join yarn
at right neck edge and complete to match left side.

Sleeves

CO 22(24)(24)(26) sts and knit
10 rows.

Continued on page 171

Argyle Damask Vest

Design by Kathleen Power Johnson

*The effect of argyle in one color highlights
an angular-shaped vest.*

Experience Level
Advanced****

Size
Women's small(medium)
(large) Instructions are
given for smallest size,
with larger sizes in parentheses. When only 1 num-
ber is given, it applies to
all sizes.

Finished Measurements
Chest: 40(42)(44) inches
Length: 17½(17¾)(18½)
inches

Materials
- Peaches & Creme 100
  percent cotton worsted
  weight yarn from
  Elmore-Pisgah Inc. (840
  yds/16 oz per cone):
  1(1)(2) cones persim-
  mon #33
- Size 5 (3.75mm) 36-inch
  circular needle
- Size 7 (4.5mm) needles
  or size needed to obtain
  gauge
- Stitch markers
- Tapestry needle
- 1 (¾-inch) button
  #10576 from JHB
  International Inc.

Gauge
19 sts and 27 rows = 4 inches/
10cm in patt with larger ndls

To save time, take time to
check gauge.

Pattern Stitch
(multiple of 16 sts)

Row 1 (RS): *P1, k5, p1, k1,
p1, k5, p2, rep from * across.

Row 2 and rem WS rows:
K the knit sts and p the purl sts.

Row 3: *P2, [k3, p1] twice,
k3, p3, rep from * across.

Row 5: *P3, k1, p1, k5, p1,
k1, p4, rep from * across.

Row 7: *P4, k7, p5, rep
from * across.

Row 9: *P2, k1, p2, k5, p2,
k1, p3, rep from * across.

Row 11: *P1, k1, p4, k3,
p4, k1, p2, rep from * across.

Row 13: *[K1, p6] twice,
k1, p1, rep from * across.

Row 15: *P15, k1, rep from
* across.

Row 17: Rep Row 13.

Row 19: Rep Row 11.

Row 21: Rep Row 9.

Row 23: Rep Row 7.

Row 25: Rep Row 5.

Row 27: Rep Row 3.

Row 29: Rep Row 1.

Row 31: *[K7, p1] twice,
rep from * across.

Row 32: K the knit sts and
p the purl sts.

Rep Rows 1–32 for patt.

Back
With larger ndls, CO
94(100)(104) sts and work in
St st until piece meas 9(9¼)
(9½) inches from beg.

Shape underarms
BO 7 sts at beg of next 2 rows,
then dec 1 st each side [eor]
7(10)(11) times.

Work even on rem 66(66)
(68) sts until back meas
17½(17¾) (18½) inches from
beg. Work across 19(19)(20)
sts and place on holder, BO
center 28 sts for back neck,
work rem 19(19) (20) sts and
place on holder.

Left Front
CO 1 st.

Row 1 (RS): [P1, yo, p1] in
same st. (3 sts)

Row 2: K1, k1b, k1.

Referring to Chart A, (on
page 170), beg with Row 3, at
end of every RS row (front
edge), [{CO 2 sts} twice, {inc 1
st} once] 5 times, then [CO 2
sts] twice, [inc 1 st] once.

At the same time, at end of
every WS row (underarm
edge), [CO 3 sts] 8 times,
then [CO 4(9)(14) sts] once.
Work underarm edge even
from this point.

Shape front neck
When front edge incs are
completed, beg with next RS
row, shape front neck by dec 1
st at front edge [every 4th
row] 24 times.

Continued on page 170

Comfy Cozy Tunic

Design by Ann E. Smith

This tunic is knit from side to side with a border attached at the top and bottom. The yoke is worked in one piece. What fun!

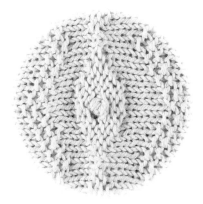

Experience Level
Intermediate***

Size
Women's small(medium)(large)(extra-large) Instructions are given for smallest size with larger sizes in parentheses. When only 1 number is given, it applies to all sizes.

Finished Measurements
Chest: 43½(46)(48)(50¼) inches
Length: Approximately 30½ inches

Materials
- Aunt Lydia's Denim Quick 75 percent cotton/25 percent acrylic Crochet Thread from Coats & Clark (400 yds/8 oz per ball): 4(4)(5)(5) balls milk #1002
- Size 6 (4mm) needles or size needed to obtain gauge
- Stitch markers
- Tapestry needle

Gauge
20 sts and 28 rows (14 ridges) = 4 inches/10cm in garter st
 To save time, take time to check gauge.

Pattern Notes
Beg with center section, working patt from Chart A. Center portion is worked from side to side.

 Yoke is worked in 1 piece from back to shoulders, then divided for neck. Sides are then worked with separate balls of yarn.

Special Abbreviations
Make Bobble (MB): In next st, k1, [k1, yo] 4 times, then pass first 8 sts over last st.

 Make 1 (M1): Inc by lifting running thread bet sts on ndls; place strand on LH ndl, k1 tbl.

Pattern Stitch
Bobble Diamond
 Row 1(RS): K1, p2, *k7, p3, rep from * across, ending k7, p2, k1.

 Row 2: P1, k3, *p5, k5, rep from * across, ending p5, k3, p1.

 Row 3: K1, p4, (k3, p7) across, ending k3, p4, k1.

 Row 4: P1, k5, (p1, k9) across ending p1, k5, p1.

 Row 5: K1, MB, p4, (k1, p4, MB, p4) across ending k1, p4, MB, k1.

 Row 6: Rep Row 4.
 Row 7: Rep Row 3.
 Row 8: Rep Row 2.
 Row 9: Rep Row 1.

Back
Center Section

Continued on page 172

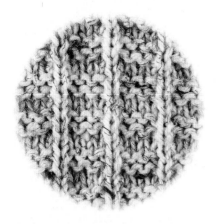

Rustic Textured Ribs

Design by Melissa Leapman

This 4-row repeat textured stitch pullover is constructed with a clever neck finish.

Experience Level
Advanced Beginner**

Size
Adult's small(medium)(large)(extra-large) Instructions are given for smallest size, with larger sizes in parentheses. When only 1 number is given, it applies to all sizes.

Finished Measurements
Chest: 39(42)(46)(49) inches

Length: 23(24)(24½)(25) inches

Materials
• Stylecraft's Rustic Aran with Wool 72 percent acrylic/20 percent wool/8 percent viscose worsted weight yarn from S.R. Kertzer Ltd. (235 yds/100g per skein): 5(5)(6)(6) skeins #3460
• Size 8 (5mm) needles or size needed to obtain gauge
• Stitch holders
• Tapestry needle

Gauge
18 sts and 28 rows = 4 inches/10cm in patt

To save time, take time to check gauge.

Pattern Stitch
Textured Rib (multiple of 4 sts + 3)

Row 1 (RS): P3, *k1, p3, rep from * across.

Row 2: K3, *p1, k3, rep from * across.

Row 3: Knit.

Row 4: Purl.

Rep Rows 1–4 for patt.

Back
CO 87(95)(103)(111) sts.

Work even in patt until piece meas 14(14½)(14½)(14½) inches from beg, ending with a WS row.

Shape armholes
At beg of row, BO [4(4)(4)(8) sts] twice, then [2(3)(3)(3) sts] twice. Dec 1 st at each edge [every row] 3(8)(7)(5) times, then [eor] 3(1)(2)(4) times. (63, 63, 71, 71 sts rem)

Continue to work even in est patt until piece meas 21(22)(22½)(23) inches from beg, ending with a WS row.

Shape neck
Work across first 8(8)(12)(12) sts, join 2nd skein of yarn and BO center 47 sts, work to end of row.

Work even on both sides at once with separate skeins of yarn until piece meas 22(23)(23½)(24) inches from beg, ending with a WS row.

Shape shoulders
At beg of row, BO [2(2)(3)(3) sts] 8 times.

Front
Work as for back until piece meas 16¾(17¾)(18¼)(18¾) inches from beg, ending with a RS row.

Shape neck
Next row (WS): Work in patt across first 31(31)(35)(35) sts, join 2nd skein of yarn and BO center st, work to end of row.

Dec row: Maintaining patt throughout, work first 22(22)(26)(26) sts, k2tog, work 7 sts; on other side of neck, work 7 sts, ssk, complete row.

Continue to work in patt, dec at each neck edge as above [eor] 11 more times, then [every 4th row] 3 times. (16, 16, 20, 20 sts rem each side)

Work even until fronts meas same as back at shoulders.

Shape shoulders as for back, then continue to work even on rem 8 sts on each side until pieces meet at center back when slightly stretched. Sl sts to holders.

Sleeves
CO 39 sts.

Work in patt, inc 1 st each side [every 6th row] 0(0)(0)(11) times, [every 8th row] 0(11)(14)(6) times, [every 10th row] 8(2)(0)(0) times, then [every 12th row] 2(0)(0)(0)

Continued on page 171

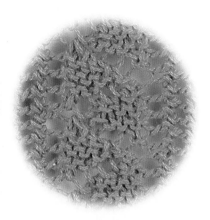

Mexican Lace Cardigan

Design by Lois S. Young

Take a lace border to the extreme with a romantic cardigan.

Gauge
24 sts and 32 rows = 4 inches/ 10cm in st st.

To save time, take time to check gauge.

Pattern Notes
For front and side edges, work first st of each RS row as sl 1 purlwise and first 2 sts of each WS row as sl 1 knitwise, k1.

For side neck edges, sl first st of each RS row purlwise and first st of each WS row knitwise.

Lace is reversible. When sewing pieces tog, reverse front, neck front, sleeve edgings and side neck pieces of left side to form mirror images.

Sew lace to body pieces by overcasting stitch for stitch through chains formed by sl sts along side edges or by CO or BO sts. Sew side seams in same manner.

Right Back
CO 44(50)(56) sts.

Rows 1–3: Sl 1, k to end.

Work back and forth in St st, working edges as in Pattern Notes. Continue until piece meas 9¼(10¼)(11¼) inches (approximately 75(83)(91) rows), or 2¾ inches less than desired length to underarm, ending with a WS row.

Shape armhole
At beg of row, BO 10(11)(12) sts for underarm, then dec [every RS row] 9(10)(11) times by k2, ssk, k to end of row. (25, 29, 33 sts)

Continue in St st until armhole meas 4⅛(4⅝)(5⅛) inches above dec sts. (approximately 35, 39, 43 rows)

On next WS row, BO 19(21) (23) sts for neck edge. Work back and forth in St st for 28 rows, working neck edge sts as in Pattern Notes. BO rem 6(8)(10) sts.

Left Back
Work to match right back to underarm.

Shape armhole
On next WS row, BO 10(11) (12) sts for underarm, then dec [every RS row] 9(10)(11) times by k to last 4 sts, k2tog, k2. (25, 29, 33 sts)

Continue in St st until armhole meas 4⅛ (4⅝)(5⅛) inches above dec sts. (approximately 35, 39, 43 rows)

On next RS row, BO 19(21) (23) sts for neck edge. Work back and forth in St st for 28 rows, working neck edge sts as in Pattern Notes. BO rem 6(8)(10) sts.

Right and Left Fronts
Work to match right and left backs, but BO for front neck 2(4)(6) rows after armhole decs are finished. Work back and forth on rem sts for 44 rows before BO.

Continued on page 173

Chevron Vest

Design by Barbara Venishnick

Four pieces shaped and worked on the diagonal come together in a flattering vest.

Experience Level
Intermediate***

Size
Women's small(medium) (large) Instructions are given for smallest size, with larger sizes in parentheses. When only 1 number is given, it applies to all sizes.

Finished Measurements
Chest: 40(44)(48) inches
Length: 22(23)(24) inches

Materials
- Bluefaced Leicester 100 percent wool worsted weight yarn from Berroco Inc. (103 yds/50g per ball): 8(9)(10) balls sage #7007
- Size 6 (4mm) straight and 29-inch circular needles
- Stitch holders
- Stitch markers
- Tapestry needle
- 1 (1¾-inch) pewter clasp

Gauge
20 sts and 32 rows = 4 inches/ 10cm in patt

To save time, take time to check gauge.

Pattern Notes
Vest is made in 4 sections. Sections begin at side seam vent and are worked diagonal-

ly to top. All are worked alike until bottom edge is completed, then shaping varies from that point.

Keep 1 selvage st at each edge of pieces in St st throughout, working patt and all shaping inside selvages.

Pattern Stitch
(worked on an odd number of sts)

Rows 1 and 3 (RS): Knit.
Row 2: Purl.
Rows 4 and 6: Knit.
Row 5: *K2tog, yo, rep from * to last st, end k1.

Rep Rows 1–6 for patt.

Left Back
Bottom and side edge
CO 19 sts and work Rows 1 and 2 of patt.

Beg with Row 3, inc 1 st at each edge every RS row until there are 73(79)(85) sts on ndl, ending with Row 2 of patt.

Center and side edges
Beg with patt Row 3, dec 1 st at beg and inc 1 st at end every RS row. Complete Rows 3–6, then work [Rows 1–6] twice. (st count does not change)

Shape underarm
Beg with patt Row 1, dec 1 st at beg and end [every RS row] 10 times, ending with Row 2 of patt. (53, 59, 65 sts rem)

Beg with patt Row 3, dec 1 st at beg and inc 1 st at end every RS row. Complete Rows 4–6, then work [Rows 1–6] 10 times. (st count does not change)

Shape shoulder
Beg with patt Row 1, dec 1 st at beg and end [every RS row] 8 times, ending with Row 4 of patt. (37, 43, 49 sts rem)

Continue to work back in est patt, continuing decs every RS row until 5 sts rem, ending with a WS row.

Next row (RS): K1, k3tog, k1. Turn and p3tog. Cut yarn, pull end through rem st.

Right Front
Work as left back until 37(43) (49) sts rem. Sl sts on holder for front neck.

Right Back
Work bottom and side edge as for left back.

Center and side edges
Beg with patt Row 3, inc 1 st

Continued on page 174

Swing Band Pullover

Design by Lois S. Young

A crisp cotton yarn highlights the intense texture of this challenging pullover.

Experience Level
Advanced****

Size
Women's small(medium) (large) Instructions are given for smallest size, with larger sizes in parentheses. When only 1 number is given, it applies to all sizes.

Finished Measurements
Chest: 36(42)(48) inches

Side to underarm: 13(14)(15) inches

Armhole depth: 8½(9)(9½) inches

Total sleeve length: 18¾(19¾)(20¾) inches

Materials
- JCA/Reynolds, Inc. Saucy 100 percent cotton worsted weight yarn from JCA Inc. (185 yds/100g skein): 8(9)(10) skeins rose #395
- Size 6 (4mm) straight and 16-inch circular needles or size needed to obtain gauge
- Stitch holders
- Tapestry needle

Gauge
23 sts and 30 rows = 4 inches/ 10cm in patt

To save time, take time to check gauge.

Special Abbreviations
Make 1 (M1): Inc by making a backward loop over right ndl.

SSP: Sl 2 sts individually as if to k, return them to left ndl in this position, p2tog tbl.

Back
CO 109(127)(145) sts.

Work Rows 1–50 of patt from Chart A,

Work [Rows 51–62] 4(4)(5) times, [Rows 51–54] 0(1)(1) time and [Rows 55–58] 0(1) (0) time.

Shape armholes
Continuing in patt, BO 9 sts at beg of next 2 rows. (91, 109, 127 sts)

Work in est patt until there are 8(9)(10) zigzag bands above ribbing, ending with Row 62. Work Rows 63–88.

BO 21(24)(27) sts at beg of next 2 rows. Place rem 49(61)(73) sts on holder for neck. Break yarn, set aside.

Front

Work to match back, ending with Row 82.

Shape left shoulder

Continuing in est patt, work across first 38(41)(44) sts, turn; yo, work back. Work 32(35)(38) sts, turn; yo, work back. Work 26(29)(32) sts, turn work. Work 5 sts, then BO rem 21(24)(27) sts, working each yo tog with following st as ssk if st is knit and ssp if st is purl.

Shape right shoulder

Sl next 49(61)(73) sts to other ndl. Attach yarn at armhole edge and work shoulder as mirror image of left shoulder. When working BO row, work each yo as k2tog or p2tog, depending on following st. Place rem 49(61)(73) sts on holder for front neck. Set aside.

Sleeves

CO 41(47)(53) sts.

Work Rows 1–18 from Chart B. Referring to chart, inc 8 (10)(12) sts on Row 19. (49, 57, 65 sts)

Continue to work patt from Chart B, rep Rows 47–58 to top of sleeve. At the same time, beg on next RS row, inc 1 st after first st and before last st [every 4th row] 23(15) (11) times, then [every 6th row] 0(7)(11) times. (95, 101, 109 sts)

Work even until sleeve meas 18¾(19¾)(20¾) inches. BO all sts.

Finishing

Sew shoulder seams. Sew top of sleeve into armhole. Sew underarm edges of sleeve into bottom of armhole and then sew rem part of sleeve seam.

Neck band

Remove neck sts from holders and place on circular ndl. Mark beg of rnd.

Beg working rib patt as est in rnds, working p2tog at each shoulder to reduce 4 p sts to 3. Work neck ribbing for a total of 6 rnds. BO in patt. ❖

CHART A

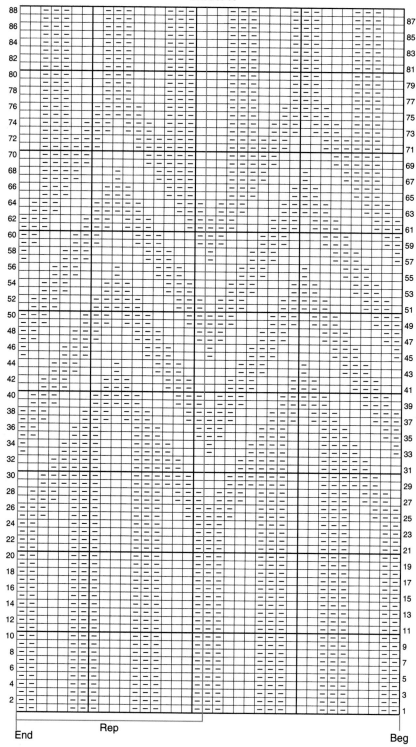

Rep

End   Beg

CHART B

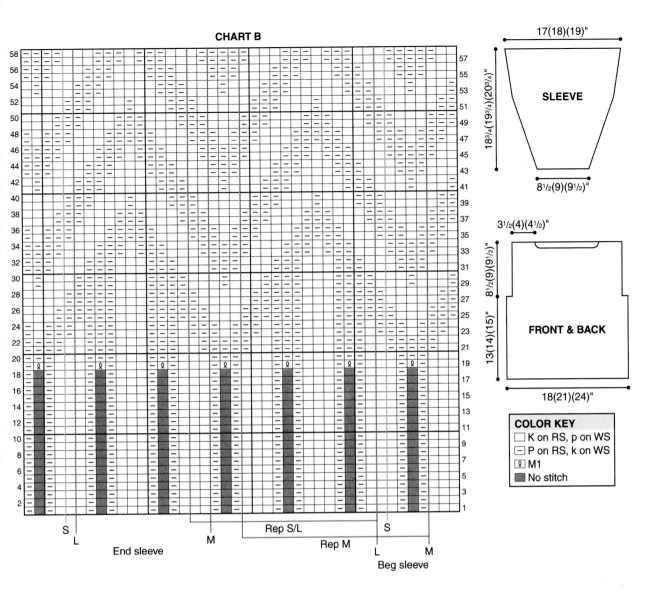

Chart row numbers (left): 58, 56, 54, 52, 50, 48, 46, 44, 42, 40, 38, 36, 34, 32, 30, 28, 26, 24, 22, 20, 18, 16, 14, 12, 10, 8, 6, 4, 2

Chart row numbers (right): 57, 55, 53, 51, 49, 47, 45, 43, 41, 39, 37, 35, 33, 31, 29, 27, 25, 23, 21, 19, 17, 15, 13, 11, 9, 7, 5, 3, 1

S
L
End sleeve
M
Rep S/L
Rep M
S
L
M
Beg sleeve

17(18)(19)"
SLEEVE
18¾(19¾)(20¾)"
8½(9)(9½)"

3½(4)(4½)"
8½(9)(9½)"
13(14)(15)"
FRONT & BACK
18(21)(24)"

COLOR KEY

☐	K on RS, p on WS
⊟	P on RS, k on WS
℧	M1
▩	No stitch

Strips of Lace Vest

Continued from page 144

patt without inc, dec at end of every RS row until 1 st rem. Fasten off.

Strip E

CO 20 sts and work as D, reversing shaping by M1 at end of every RS row and k2tog at end of every WS row.

Strip F

Make 1

Ladder Lace

CO 23 sts.

Row 1 (RS): *Ssk, yo, k1, yo, k2tog, k1, rep from *, end ssk, yo, k1, yo, k2tog.

Row 2: Purl.

Rep Rows 1 and 2 for patt until piece meas 23(24)(25)(26) inches from beg. Work 5 rows of garter st, then BO all sts.

Finishing

Referring to schematic, sew strips tog as shown, overlapping by ¼ inch. For left front, reverse right front layout, using strips E, A and B.

Tie

CO 4 sts and work back and forth in St st until tie meas 36 inches. BO all sts. On back, thread tie through center set of eyelets nearest waist-line, tie ends in a bow. ❖

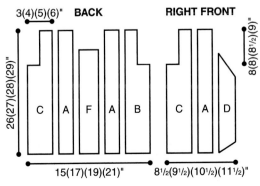

3(4)(5)(6)" **BACK**   **RIGHT FRONT**
8(8)(8½)(9)"
26(27)(28)(29)"
C A F A B   C A D
15(17)(19)(21)"   8½(9½)(10½)(11½)"

strips each patts B and C. Beg with 5 rows garter st, then work 192 rows of patt. Do not BO; place all sts on holders.

Right Front

Work 1 strip each patts A, B, and C as for back. Work 1 strip patt A 144 rows long for center front. Do not BO; place all sts on holders.

Left Front

Make strips as for right front.

Sleeve

CO 64 sts. Work in patt D for 8 inches, inc 1 st on each side [every 6th row] 10 times. (84 sts)

BO all sts. Sew side seam.

Finishing

Referring to Fig. 1 and using a crochet hook, join strips, taking care to match patts on front and back strips.

FIG. 1

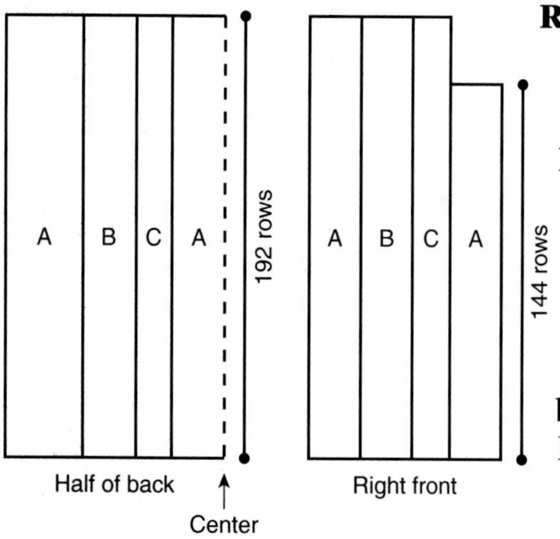

```
+---+---+-+---+    +---+---+-+---+
|   |   | |   |    |   |   | |   |
|   |   | |   |    |   |   | |   |
| A | B |C| A |    | A | B |C| A |
|   |   | |   |    |   |   | |   |
|   |   | |   |    |   |   | |   |
+---+---+-+---+    +---+---+-+---+
  Half of back       Right front
       ↑
     Center
```

192 rows

144 rows

BO front and back shoulder sts tog as follows:

Hold ndls containing shoulder sts parallel, right sides tog; with 3rd ndl, k first st on front and back ndls tog, *k next st on both ndls tog, BO 1, rep from * until all sts are worked, fasten off. Rep for 2nd shoulder.

Button band

Pick up and k 75 sts along left front edge.

Rows 1–10: Knit.

BO all sts.

Buttonhole band

Pick up and k 75 sts from right front edge.

Rows 1–5: Knit.

Row 6: K6, *yo, ssk, k8, rep from *, end k4. (7 buttonholes)

Rows 7–10: Knit.

BO all sts.

Neck band

Pick up and k 140 sts around neck, including sts on holders.

Rows 1–6: Knit.

Row 7: K3, yo, ssk, k135.

Rows 8–11: Knit.

BO all sts firmly.

Lower edge

With crochet hook and WS facing, work 1 row of sc around bottom edge. Fasten off. Set in sleeves.

Block sweater to size. Sew buttons across from buttonholes. ❖

into fabric, you will need to do a regular [k1, ssk] dec and work rem of row in patt, pairing yo's and ssk's.

For right front armhole shaping, because st patt slants to left, all right-sloping shaping will be performed on last 3 sts of row, by using a [k2tog, k1] dec. Note that last st of a RS row will always be a k st, thus keeping selvage in St st. However, because yo's and ssk's must be paired, sometimes it will be necessary to "squeeze" yo and ssk of patt tog. Thus, if it is not possible to work [yo, k3, ssk] before 3-st armhole dec, you may need to work [yo, k2 (or k1), ssk], or simply to omit yo altogether.

Join yarn, [dec for left armhole (see notes above), work in patt across, dec for right armhole and making adjustments to st patt as needed at end of row. Purl 1 row.] 11(9)(7)(10) times. (71, 81, 90, 90 sts)

Divide for neck

Dec for left armhole, work across until there are 21(26)(29)(29) sts on RH ndl, place sts on holder for left front. BO number of sts necessary so that next st in patt should be a yo (probably 4, 6, 6, 6 sts), k that st, work in patt across, dec for right armhole, making adjustments to st patt as needed at end of row. Purl 1 row.

Shape right neck

Right neck will be shaped by omitting a yo at beg of row, as described in left front armhole

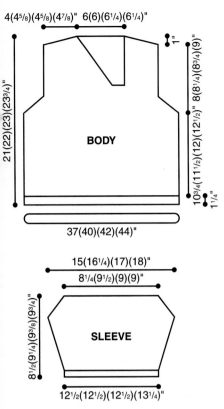

4(4⅝)(4⅝)(4⅞)" 6(6)(6¼)(6¼)"

21(22)(23)(23¾)"

BODY

1"

10¾(11½)(12)(12½)" 8(8¼)(8¾)(9)"

1¼"

37(40)(42)(44)"

15(16¼)(17)(18)"
8¼(9½)(9)(9)"

8½(9¼)(9⅜)(9¾)"

SLEEVE

12½(12½)(12½)(13¼)"

shaping note above. Therefore, as you look at RS of sweater, ready to knit, next st in patt should be a yo. If not, adjust number of BO sts.

Left neck edge will rem straight— on some rows you will need to "squeeze" yo's and ssk's, or omit yo, as described in right front armhole shaping note above. Make similar adjustments on right front armhole once that armhole shaping is complete.

When left front armhole shaping is complete, bring sts into patt on right edge of fabric by using a M1 inc (instead of a yo) to accompany later ssk dec until there are enough sts to work a complete rep of

patt plus 1 selvage st.

*K4, ssk (this ssk should line up with others in patt), work in patt across, dec for right arm-hole for sizes M, L and XL only and making adjustments to patt as needed at end of row. Purl 1 row.

Rep from * for neck shaping for all sizes and for armhole dec for sizes M(L)(XL) only until 12(12) (14)(16) armhole dec have been made, then continue neck shaping only until piece meas 20(21)(22)(22¾) inches from beg, ending with a RS row.

Shape right shoulder

Continue neck shaping and BO 7(7)(7)(8) sts at beg of next 3(2)(2)(3) WS rows, and 0(9)(9)(0) sts at beg of following WS row.

Note: *All neck shaping should be finished at same time shoulder BO is completed.*

Shape left front neck

Place left neck sts back on ndl. Continue armhole decs until 21(23)(23)(24) sts rem, then work even in patt until piece meas 20(21)(22)(22¾) inches from beg, ending with a WS row.

Shape left shoulder

BO 7(7)(7)(8) sts at beg of next 3(2)(2)(3) RS rows, and 0(9)(9) (0) sts at beg of follow-ing RS row.

Back

Place 94(99)(105)(110) sts for back on ndl. Work armhole dec [every RS row] 12(12)(14)(16) times. (70, 75, 77, 78 sts)

Work even in patt until piece meas 21(22)(22)(22¾) inches from beg, ending with a WS row.

Shape shoulders

At beg of row, BO [7(7)(7)(8) sts] 6(4)(4)(6) times, and [0(9)(9)(0) sts] 0(2)(2)(0) times. BO rem 28(29)(31)(30) sts.

Sleeve

CO 63(63)(63)(67) sts.

Row 1 (RS): P3(3)(3)(5), [yo, ssk, k3, p6] 5 times, yo, ssk, K3, p0(0)(0)(2).

Row 2: K0(0)(0)(2), [p5, k6] 5 times, p5, k3(3)(3)(5).

Rows 3–8: [Rep Rows 1 and 2] 3 times.

Row 9: K3(3)(3)(5), [yo, ssk, k9] 5 times, yo, ssk, k3(3)(3)(5).

Row 10: Purl.

Rep Rows 9 and 10 for patt, *at the same time,* inc 1 st each side [eor] 0(0)(3)(7) times, [every 4th row] 0(8)(8)(5) times, and [every 6th row] 6(1)(0)(0) times, working new sts in St st. End with a WS row. (75, 81, 85, 91 sts)

Shape sleeve cap

Maintaining est patt, BO 0(1)(0)(1) st at beg of next 2 rows and 2 sts at beg of next 16(16)(20)(22) rows. (43, 47, 45, 45 sts rem)

BO all sts.

Finishing

Sew shoulder seams. Set in sleeves and sew sleeve seams. With crochet hook, single cro-chet around neck. ❖

Argyle Diamond Vest

Continued from page 155

Shape underarm

Continuing to work front shaping, when underarm meas 9(9¼)(9½) inches, at beg of next RS row, BO [7 sts] once, then [2 sts] 0(2)(3) times. Dec 1 st at armhole edge [eor] 9(10)(12) times.

When front and underarm shapings are completed, work even in est patt until front meas 18¼(18½)(19¼) inches. Place shoulder sts on holder.

Right Front

Work as for left front, reversing shaping. Working 3 sts in from edge, make buttonhole on last front inc row by BO 2 sts, then CO 2 sts on next row.

Finishing

Sl shoulder sts to ndls and BO sts tog as follows:

Hold ndls containing shoulder sts parallel, right sides tog; with 3rd ndl, k first st on front and back ndls tog, *k next st on both ndls tog, BO 1, rep from * until all sts are worked, fasten off. Rep for 2nd shoulder.

Sew side seams.

Border

With smaller circular ndl and

CHART A

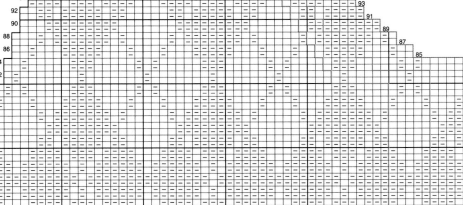

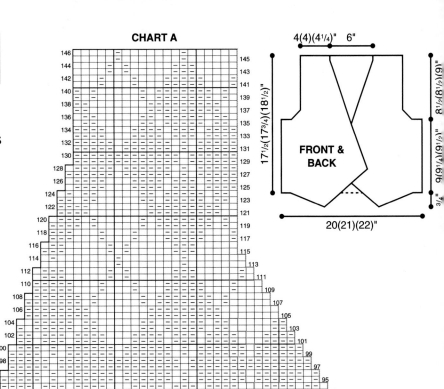

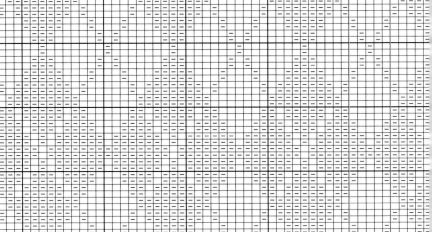

FRONT & BACK

20(21)(22)"

STITCH KEY

☐ K on RS, p on WS

⊟ P on RS, k on WS

RS facing, beg at side seam, pick up and k 3 sts for every 4 sts or rows around outside and front edges of vest, pM at each vest point. Join and work in rnds.

Rnd 1: Purl, inc 1 st on each side of markers.

Rnd 2: Purl.

BO all sts.

Armhole border

Beg at underarm, pick up and k sts around armhole, work as above, omitting incs.

Sew button on left front to match buttonhole. ❖

Patchwork Vest
Continued from page 150

Finishing

Sew shoulder seams.

Neck band

With 16-inch circular ndl, join yarn at left shoulder seam, pick up and k 18 sts along left neck edge, k across sts from front neck holder, pick up and k 18 sts along right neck edge, and 29(30)(33) sts across back neck.

Join and k 8 rnds. BO all sts.

Sleeve cap

Place markers 4 inches down from shoulder seam on front and back.

With RS facing, using 16-inch circular ndl, pick up and k 36 sts bet markers, turn.

Working in garter st, [knit 1 row, pick up and k 2 sts from armhole edge at end of row, turn] 6 times. (48 sts)

Knit across all sts, pick up and k around rem of armhole at a rate of 1 st for every row or st. Knit 1 rnd, then BO all sts knitwise.

Block lightly. ❖

Rustic Textured Ribs
Continued from page 158

times. (59, 65, 67, 73 sts)

Work even in patt until sleeve meas 16½(16½)(17)(17½) inches from beg, ending with a WS row.

Shape cap

BO 4(4)(4)(8) sts at beg of next 2 rows, then dec 1 st each side [every 4th row] 7(4)(4)(6) times, then [eor] 2(8)(8)(4) times.

BO 3 sts at beg of next 4 rows. BO rem 21(21)(23)(25) sts.

Finishing

Sew shoulder seams. Sew sides of back neck band to neckline. Graft ends of neck band tog at center back of neck.

Set in sleeves. Sew sleeve and body underarm seams, leaving bottom 3½ inches of side seams open for side slits. ❖

Lilac Bouclé Sweater
Continued from page 152

Continuing in St st, inc 1 st at each edge [every 4th row] 11(12)(12)(13) times. (44, 48, 48, 52 sts)

Work even until sleeve meas 17(17½)(18)(18½) inches or desired length from beg. BO all sts.

Finishing

Sew left shoulder seam.

Neck band

With RS facing, join yarn at right back shoulder. Pick up and k 5 sts along right back neck edge, 12(14)(14)(16) sts across back neck, 5 sts along left back neck edge, 7 sts along right front neck edge, 8(10)(10)(12) sts across front neck and 7 sts along right front neck edge. (44, 48, 48, 52 sts)

Knit 9 rows. BO all sts loosely. Sew right shoulder seam.

Place markers on body edge 9¾(10½)(10½)(11½) inches from shoulder seam. Set sleeves bet markers. Sew sleeve and body underarm seams.

Cowl

CO 60 sts and work in garter st for 13 inches. BO all sts.

Sew seam. ❖

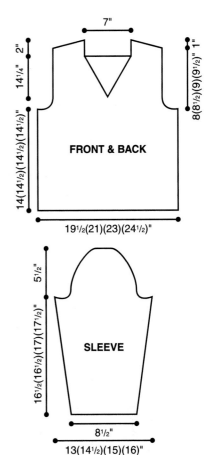

7"

2"

14¼"

8(8½)(9)(9½)" 1"

14(14½)(14½)(14½)"

FRONT & BACK

19½(21)(23)(24½)"

5½"

16½(16½)(17)(17½)"

SLEEVE

8½"

13(14½)(15)(16)"

CO 83 sts. Purl 1 row.

Working patt from Chart A, beg with Row 3(9)(5)(1) and work through Row 10, then rep [Rows 1–10] 2(3)(3)(3) times. Work Rows 11–44, then [Rows 1–44] once, [Rows 1–21] once. Work [Rows 22–31] 2(3)(3)(3) times, rep Rows 22–29(Rows 22 and 23)(Rows 22–27)(Rows 22–31). Purl 1 row. BO all sts knitwise.

Lower Border

CO 109(115)(121)(127) sts. Purl 1 row. Beg and ending as indicated for size, work Rows 1–10 of patt from Chart B.

Picot BO

BO 2 sts, *return last st to LH ndl, CO 2 sts, BO 4 sts, rep from * across, ending BO rem st(s). With picots just made as lower edge, join this piece to lower edge of center section.

Upper Border

Work as for lower border, ending with Row 10. BO loosely and knitwise. Join this piece to top edge of center section.

Front

Work as for back.

Yoke

CO 109(115)(121)(127) sts.

Work in garter st (k every row) until piece meas 7 inches from beg, ending with a WS row.

Divide for neck and shoulders

K first 38(40)(42)(44) sts, join a new strand of yarn and BO center 33(35)(37)(39) sts, k to end. Working both sides at once with separate balls of yarn, k 7 rows.

Shape neck

Row 1: K across to last st, M1, k1; for second side, k1, M1, k across.

Rows 2–6: Knit.

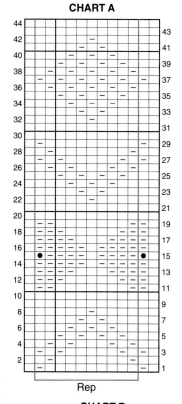

CHART A

Rep

CHART B

Rep

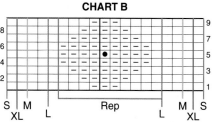

Rows 7–12: Rep Rows 1–6.

Row 13: Rep Row 1. (41, 43, 45, 47 sts for each front)

Continue to work in garter st, inc as est [eor] 19 times. (60, 62, 64, 66 sts)

K3 rows. BO loosely and knitwise.

Join yoke to front

With RS facing and holding back neck of yoke toward you with body beneath, sew yoke to body, lapping first 11(9)(7)(5) sts of right yoke over first 11(9)(7)(5) sts of left yoke.

Sleeves

Beg at top, CO 81(85)(91)(95) sts. Knit 5 rows.

Dec row (RS): K1, k2tog, k across to last 3 sts, k2tog, k1.

Working in garter st, rep dec

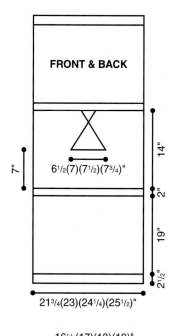

FRONT & BACK

7"

14"

6½(7)(7½)(7¾)"

2"

19"

2½"

21¾(23)(24¼)(25½)"

16¼(17)(18)(19)"

14"

2"

SLEEVE

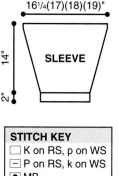

STITCH KEY
- ☐ K on RS, p on WS
- ⊟ P on RS, k on WS
- ⦿ MB

row [every 6th row] 13(8)(4)(1) times more, then [every 4th row] 0(7)(13)(17) times. (53, 53, 55, 57 sts rem)

Continue to work even until sleeve meas 14 inches from beg, ending with a RS row. Purl next row.

Working from Chart B, beg with Row 1, k1(1)(2)(3), pM, work patt rep across, pM, end k2(2)(3)(4). Continue as est, working patt rep bet markers through completion of chart. Rep Picot BO as for lower border.

Finishing

Mark center side edge of yoke. PM 8½(9)(9½)(10) inches each side of center marker. Set in sleeves bet markers.

Sew sleeve and body underarm seams. ❖

Mexican Lace Cardigan

Continued from page 161

Lace Strips

Using larger ndl, CO 14 sts.

Set up and finishing row: Sl 1 purlwise, k13.

Sleeves

For bottom lace band, work set up row once. Work [Rows 1–10 of Chart A] 6 times, then work [Rows 1–5] 0(0)(1) time. BO knitwise on WS.

Pick up 44(52)(58) sts along edge of lace. The approximate rate will be [pick up and k 1 st, * yo, pick up and k 3(2)(2) sts, rep from *].

Next row (WS): Knit.

Work back and forth in St st, inc 1 st after first 2 sts of row and before last 2 sts of row [every 4th row] 18(20)(21) times. (80, 92, 100 sts)

Work even until sleeve meas 17½ (17¾)(18¼) inches, or desired length to underarm.

Shape cap

BO 10(11)(12) sts for underarm at beg of next 2 rows, then dec 1 st each side [every RS row] 9(10)(11) times. (42, 50, 54 sts)

Work even for 15(15)(21) rows. Dec 1 st each side [every RS row] 7(10)(10) times. (28, 30, 34 sts)

At beg of row, BO [3 sts] 4 times, [3(3)(4) sts] twice, BO rem 10(12)(14) sts.

With RS of garment facing, pick up and k 1 st for each edge st of lace along bottom of sleeve. BO knitwise on WS to give edge stability.

Center Back Insert

[Work set up row] 3 times. Work Rows 1–10 of Chart A until number of edge sts on lace is 2

CHART A

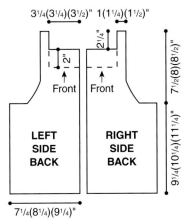

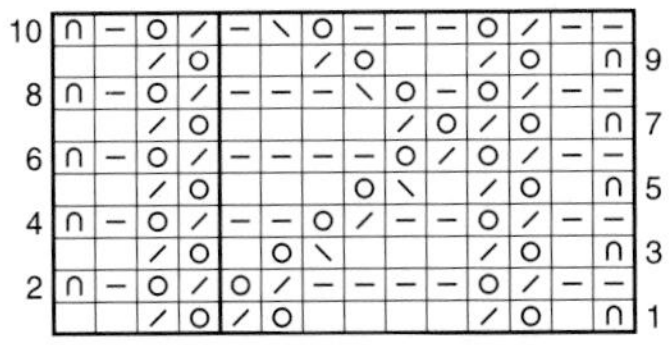

STITCH KEY
- ☐ K on RS, p on WS
- ⊟ P on RS, k on WS
- ⋒ Sl 1 as if to p
- ⊙ Yo
- ⧄ Ssk
- ⧅ P2tog

3¼(3¼)(3½)"   1(1¼)(1½)"

2¼

Front   Front

2"

7½(8)(8½)"

9¼(10¼)(11¼)"

LEFT SIDE BACK   **RIGHT SIDE BACK**

7¼(8¼)(9¼)"

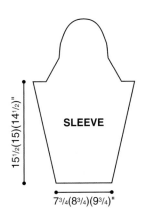

SLEEVE

15½(15)(14½)"

7¾(8¾)(9¾)"

less than number of edge sts on center back. [Work finishing row] 3 times. BO all sts.

Overcast lace insert to center back edges.

Neck Back Edging

Work set up row once. Work Rows 1–10 of Chart A until number of edge sts on lace is 1 less than number of edge sts on neck back. Work finishing row once. BO all sts.

Overcast lace insert to neck and side neck edges.

Front Band Lace Edges

[Work set up row] 3 times. Work Rows 1–10 of Chart A until number of edge sts on lace is 2 less than number of edge sts on center front, including sts of front band. [Work finishing row] 3 times. BO all sts.

Overcast lace insert to center front edge. Rep for other center front, turning lace over so mirror image of patt is formed.

Neck Front Edgings

Work set up row once. Work Rows 1–10 of Chart A until number of edge sts on lace is 2 less than number of edge sts on neck front, including sts of lace edge. [Work finishing row] 3 times. BO all sts.

Overcast lace insert to center front edge. Rep for other center front, turning lace over so mirror image of patt is formed.

Sew shoulder seams.

Neck Side Edgings

Work set up row once. Work Rows 1–10 of Chart A until number of edge sts on lace is 1 less than number of edge sts on neck side. Work finishing row once. BO all sts.

Overcast lace insert to neck edging and side neck edges. Rep for other front, turning lace over so mirror image of patt is formed.

Finishing and Bottom Band

Set in sleeves by sewing from underarm BO to shoulder, gather sleeve sts slightly at shoulder. Sew underarm seams. Sew sleeve seams.

Overcast front and back seams.

For bottom bands, [work set up row] 3 times. Work [Rows 1–10 of Chart A] 31(34)(37) times. [Work finishing row] 3 times. BO all sts knitwise on WS.

Overcast band to bottom of sweater working through each edge st of band but skipping every 3rd st on St st portion of body.

With RS of garment facing, pick up and k 1 st for each edge st of lace along bottom of sweater. BO knitwise on WS to give edge stability.

With RS of garment facing, pick up and k 1 st for each edge st of lace along fronts and neck of sweater. Work corner st of center fronts as [pick up 1, yo, pick up 1]. At side neck corners, skip corner st. BO knitwise on WS to give edge stability.

Button loop

Pick up 1 st at top right corner of front, leaving 6-inch tail. Use tail and working yarn, *CO 1 st, pull st on ndl over this CO st, rep from * 5 times or desired length of button loop. Using both strands of yarn, pick up 1 st along front edge, about 3 edge sts below other end of loop. Pull st on ndl over picked up st, fasten off. Sew button to upper left corner of front. ❖

Chevron Vest

Continued from page 162

at beg and dec 1 st at end every RS row.

Complete as for left back, reversing shaping.

Left Front

Work as right back until 37(43)(49) sts rem. Sl sts on holder for front neck.

Finishing

Sew center back and shoulder seams.

Armhole border

With circular ndl and RS facing, beg at underarm edge, pick up and k 131 sts around armhole.

Knit 2 rows. BO knitwise on WS.

Back border

With circular ndl and RS facing, beg at underarm edge, pick up and k 17 sts across CO edge, pM, 90(98)(106) sts across back, pM, and 17 sts across rem CO edge. (124, 132, 140 sts)

Knit 2 rows, dec 1 st at each edge every row. BO knitwise on WS.

Front border

With circular ndl and RS facing, beg at right underarm edge, pick up and k 17 sts across CO edge, 43(48)(53) sts across bottom edge of right front, pM, 92(97)(102) sts along front edge, k 37(43)(49) front neck sts from holder, pM, pick up and k 53(57)(62) sts across back neck, pM, k 37(43)(49) front neck sts from holder, pick up and k 92(97)(102) sts along left front edge, pM, 43(48)(53) sts across bottom edge and 17 sts along CO edge.

Row 1 (WS): K2tog, k to within 1 st of first marker, inc 1, k1, sl marker, k1, inc 1, [k to within 2 sts of next marker, k2tog, sl marker, k2tog] twice, k to within 1 st of last marker, inc 1, k1, sl marker, k1, inc 1, k to last 2 sts, end k2tog.

Row 2: Rep Row 1.

BO knitwise on WS.

Sew side seams. Sew pewter clasp at bottom of neck opening. ❖

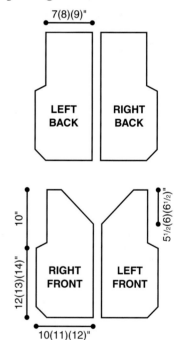

Special Thanks

*We would like to thank the talented knitting designers
whose work is featured in this collection.*

Shopper's Guide

Special thanks to the following manufacturers who provided the designers with product with which to work. To find materials listed, first check your local yarn and retail stores. If you are unable to locate a product locally, contact the manufacturers below for the closest source in your area.

Aleene's, Div. of Duncan Enterprises, 5673 E. Shields Ave., Fresno, CA 93727, (800) 237-2642

Berroco Inc., 14 Elmdale Rd., P.O. Box 367, Uxbridge, MA 01569-0367, (508) 278-2527

Brown Sheep Co., 100622 County Rd. 16, Mitchell, NE 69357, (800) 826-9136

Bryspun, 4065 W. 11th Ave. #39, Eugene, OR 97402, (800) 544-8992

C.M. Offray & Son Inc./Lion Ribbon Co. Inc., Rte. 24, Chester, NJ 07930-0601, (800) 551-LION

Cherry Tree Hill Yarns, P.O. Box 659, Barton, VT 05822, (802) 525-3311

Coats & Clark, P.O. Box 12229, Greenville, SC 29612-0229, (864) 877-8985

Dale of Norway, N16 W23390 Stoneridge Dr., Suite A, Waukesha, WI 53188, (262) 544-1996

The DMC Corp., S. Hackensack Ave., Bldg. 10A, South Kearny, NJ 07032, (973) 589-0606

Elmore-Pisgah Inc., P.O. Box 187, Spindale, NC 28160, (828) 286-3665

Euro Yarns/Knitting Fever, P.O. Box 502, Roosevelt, NY 11575

Fairfield Processing Co., P.O. Box 1130, Danbury, CT 06813, (800) 243-0989

JCA /Reynolds Inc., 35 Scales Lane, Townsend, MA 01469-1094, (978) 597-8794

JHB International, 1955 S. Quice St., Denver, CO 80231, (303) 751-8100

Lane Borgosesia, 527 South Tejon, Ste. 200, Colorado Springs, CO 80903, (800) 431-1999

Lion Brand Yarn Co., 34 W. 15th St., New York, NY 10011, (212) 243-8995

Louet Sales, P.O. Box 267, 52 East River St., Ogdensburg, NY 13669, (613) 925-4502

Plymouth Yarn Co., P.O. Box 28, Bristol, PA 19007, (215) 788-0459

S.R. Kertzer Limited, 105A

Winges Road, Woodbridge, ON, L4L 6C2, Canada, (800) 263-2354

Spinrite Yarns, Box 40, Listowel, Ontario, N4W 3H3 Canada (519) 291-3780

Steinbach Wolle, L. Steinbach GmbH, A-4311 Schwertberg, Postfach 11 Germany, 07262/41 4 31

Tahki/Stacy Charles Inc., 1059 Manhattan Ave., Brooklyn, NY 11222, (718) 389-0411

Westrim Crafts, P.O. Box 3879, Chatsworth, CA 91313, (800) 727-2727

WheelSmith Wools, 308 S. Pennsylvania Ave., P.O. Box 13, Centre Hall, PA 16828, (814) 364-2057

Yarn By Mills, Star Rte. 2, Box 28, Wallback, WV 25285

Zweigart, 121 Arthur Ave., Colonia, NJ 07067, (800) 931-4545